INTRUSION DETECTION SYSTEM

INTRUSION DETECTION SYSTEM

Parveen A.
Associate Professor,
Dept of CSE, Sathyabama Institute
of Science and Technology

R. Nivedha
Associate Professor,
Dept of CSE, Sathyabama Institute
of Science and Technology

KHANNA BOOK PUBLISHING CO. (P) Ltd.
4C/4344, Ansari Road, Darya Ganj,
New Delhi, India

Sathyabama Institute of Science and Technology
Jeppiaar Nagar, Rajiv Gandhi Salai,
Chennai, Tamilnadu, India

ISBN: 978-93-55382-47-4

INTRUSION DETECTION SYSTEM
by **Parveen A. | R. Nivedha**

First Edition: 2025

To view complete list of books, please scan the QR Code:

Published by:
Khanna Book Publishing Co. (P) Ltd.
CIN: U22110DL1998PTC095547

Visit us at: www.khannabooks.com
Write us at: contact@khannabooks.com

Printed in Bharat.

Preface

"Intrusion Detection Systems" provides a thorough introduction to the critical domain of network security, offering readers a deep understanding of IDS fundamentals and their role in protecting digital environments. This book explores how machine learning and artificial intelligence are revolutionizing IDS by enhancing threat detection capabilities.

It also delves into emerging technologies and advanced techniques, including hybrid models that address complex cyber threats. By analyzing current methodologies and future trends, readers will gain valuable insights into the research challenges shaping IDS development, preparing them to navigate this dynamic field with both theoretical expertise and practical insights.

Contents

Introduction to Intrusion Detection Systems

1

UNIT

RATIONALE

Intrusion Detection Systems (IDS) play a critical role in identifying and mitigating threats in increasingly complex network environments. This chapter provides a historical perspective on the evolution of IDS, enabling readers to understand how these systems have adapted to emerging cyber threats over time. It explores different types of IDS—signature-based, anomaly-based, and hybrid—highlighting their unique detection methodologies and applications. The comparison between IDS and Intrusion Prevention Systems (IPS) emphasizes the complementary roles they play in modern security architectures. Additionally, the chapter offers insights into various IDS deployment strategies and architectures, ensuring readers grasp the practical aspects of implementation. Metrics for evaluating IDS effectiveness are discussed to equip readers with tools for assessing system performance. A case study on enterprise-level IDS deployment further bridges theory with real-world application, making this chapter indispensable for understanding the fundamental principles and operational strategies of IDS.

OUTCOMES

- **IDS Evolution**: Understand the historical development of IDS from foundational concepts to commercial systems.
- **Types of IDS**: Learn about signature-based, anomaly-based, and hybrid IDS systems.
- **IDS vs. IPS**: Differentiate between passive IDS monitoring and proactive IPS threat prevention.
- **IDS Architectures**: Study network-based and host-based IDS architectures and their deployment strategies.
- **Evaluating IDS Effectiveness**: Use metrics like detection accuracy and false-positive rates to assess IDS performance.
- **Case Study Application**: Apply knowledge through case studies on the evolution and deployment of IDS in enterprise networks.

1.1 HISTORY AND EVOLUTION OF IDS

The evolution of Intrusion Detection Systems (IDS) can be traced back to the early 1980s, a period marked by the increasing reliance on computer networks and the corresponding rise in security threats. The foundational work in this field began with James Anderson's influential 1980 paper, "Computer Security Threat Monitoring and Surveillance," which highlighted the importance of monitoring audit trails to detect unauthorized access and misuse. This initial concept laid the groundwork for future IDS developments by emphasizing the need for proactive security measures.

1.1.1 Early Developments

By the 1990s, IDS technology began to mature as commercial solutions emerged. The introduction of Host-Based Intrusion Detection Systems (HIDS) allowed organizations to monitor individual hosts for suspicious activities, while Network-Based Intrusion Detection Systems (NIDS) provided insights into network traffic patterns. The increasing sophistication of cyber threats during this decade necessitated more robust detection mechanisms, leading to innovations in detection techniques such as signature-based detection, which relies on known patterns of malicious activity.

The late 1990s marked a turning point as organizations recognized the importance of integrating IDS into their security infrastructures. The Federal Intrusion Detection Network (FID Net), established under Presidential Decision Directive 63, exemplified government initiatives aimed at enhancing cybersecurity through advanced monitoring capabilities.

1.1.2 Recent Trends and Future Directions

In recent years, the focus has shifted towards Intrusion Prevention Systems (IPS) that not only detect but also actively block potential intrusions. This evolution reflects a growing understanding that detection alone is insufficient in combating sophisticated cyber threats. Modern IDS solutions increasingly incorporate machine learning and artificial intelligence to improve anomaly detection capabilities and adapt to evolving threat landscapes.

Moreover, the integration of IDS with other security technologies such as firewalls and Security Information and Event Management (SIEM) systems has become common practice in enterprise environments. This holistic approach enhances visibility across networks and enables faster response times to potential threats.

As cyber threats continue to evolve, ongoing research and development efforts aim to refine IDS technologies further. Emerging trends such as cloud-based IDS solutions and automated incident response mechanisms are expected to play significant roles in shaping the future of intrusion detection.

Video Resources
https://www.youtube.com/watch?v=dfVAi87BSEs

Use of ICT

Information and Communication Technology (ICT) plays a pivotal role in documenting and advancing the history and evolution of Intrusion Detection Systems (IDS). ICT enables the creation and maintenance of digital archives containing historical records and research papers on IDS development, such as early systems like IDES from the 1980s. Online libraries like IEEE Xplore and ACM Digital Library provide access to seminal works, while collaboration tools facilitate global research collaboration. ICT tools like Tableau or Python libraries help visualize the progression of IDS from signature-based systems to modern AI-driven solutions through interactive timelines and graphs. Additionally, ICT supports simulation in virtual environments for educational purposes and analysis of historical data to identify trends in IDS development. E-learning platforms offer courses on cybersecurity history, including IDS evolution, and multimedia content aids in understanding technological advancements. ICT also facilitates the dissemination of knowledge through web publishing and discussions on social media and forums, thereby driving innovation and education in the field. The evolution of IDS itself is deeply intertwined with ICT advancements, from early rule-based systems to modern AI and cloud computing integrations.

1.2 TYPES OF IDS: SIGNATURE-BASED, ANOMALY-BASED, HYBRID

Intrusion Detection Systems can be categorized into three primary types based on their detection methodologies: signature-based, anomaly-based, and hybrid systems. Each type has distinct characteristics, advantages, and limitations that make them suitable for different security environments.

1.2.1 Signature-based IDS

Signature-based IDS as given in figure 1.1 operates by comparing incoming data packets against a database of known attack signatures or patterns. This method is effective for detecting well-known threats but has notable limitations.

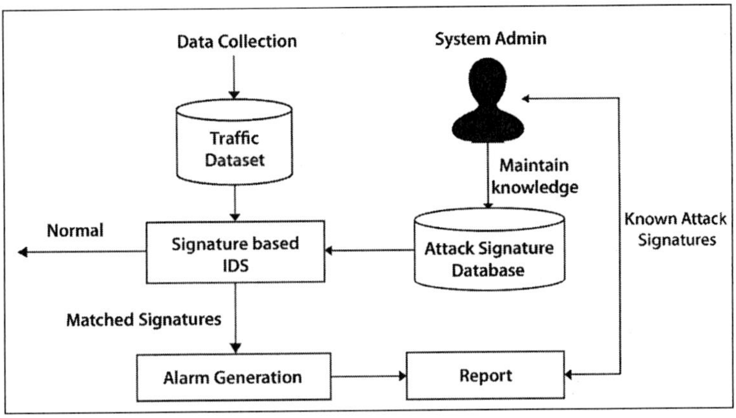

Figure 1.1: *Signature Based intrusion Detection System*

Advantages

- High accuracy in identifying known threats.
- Low false positive rates since it relies on predefined signatures.
- Efficient resource utilization as it does not require extensive computational power.

Limitations

- Ineffective against new or unknown attacks that do not have corresponding signatures.
- Requires regular updates to its signature database to remain effective.
- Vulnerable to evasion techniques where attackers modify their methods slightly to bypass detection.

Signature-based systems are commonly used in environments where known threats are prevalent, making them suitable for many traditional IT infrastructures.

1.2.2 Anomaly-based IDS

Anomaly-based IDS as given in figure 1.2 employs statistical analysis to establish a baseline of normal behavior for users or systems within an environment. It then monitors activity for deviations from this baseline.

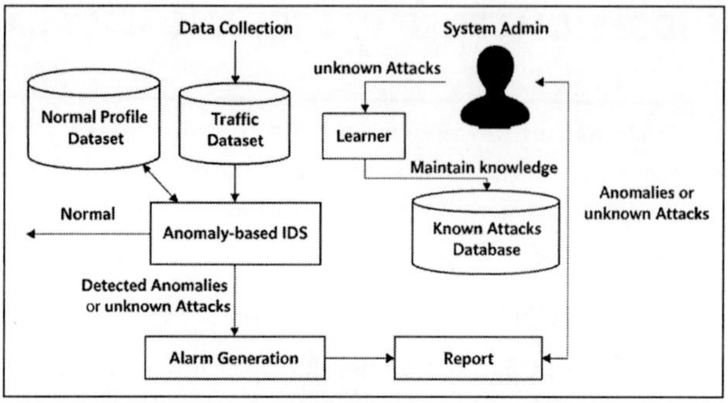

Figure 1.2.: *Anomaly Based Intrusion Detection System*

Advantages

- Capable of detecting unknown or novel attacks by identifying unusual patterns.
- Does not require prior knowledge of specific attack signatures.
- Adaptable as it can learn from new data over time using machine learning techniques.

Limitations

- Higher false positive rates due to legitimate behavior changes being flagged as anomalies.
- Requires significant computational resources for data analysis.
- Initial setup can be complex as establishing a baseline requires time and careful tuning.

Anomaly-based systems are particularly valuable in dynamic environments where user behavior may change frequently or where new threats emerge regularly.

1.2.3 Hybrid IDS

Hybrid IDS as given in figure 1.3 combines elements of both signature-based and anomaly-based detection methods. This approach aims to leverage the strengths of each system while mitigating their weaknesses.

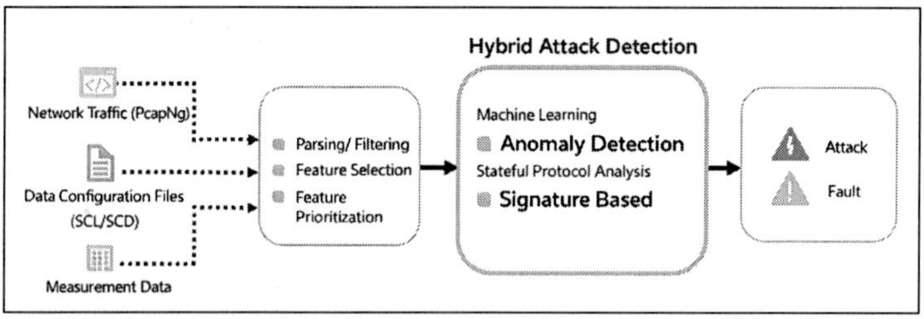

Figure 1.3.: *Hybrid Intrusion Detection System*

Advantages

- Comprehensive coverage against both known and unknown threats.
- Improved accuracy by cross-referencing detected anomalies with known signatures.
- Enhanced adaptability through machine learning techniques that refine detection capabilities over time.

Limitations

- Increased complexity in deployment and management due to multiple detection methodologies.
- Potentially higher resource requirements compared to single-method systems.
- May still experience false positives if not properly tuned.

Hybrid systems are ideal for organizations seeking robust security solutions capable of addressing diverse threat landscapes while maintaining operational efficiency.

Video Resources
https://www.perplexity.ai/search/you-tube-link-for-types-of-idsw_uak9aUQNC8uC5m.rk0mw

Use of ICT

Information and Communication Technology (ICT) plays a pivotal role in understanding the types of Intrusion Detection Systems (IDS). ICT facilitates learning through digital platforms like Coursera and YouTube, which offer courses and tutorials on Network-Based IDS (NIDS), Host-Based IDS (HIDS), and Hybrid IDS. Simulation tools such as Cisco Packet Tracer and GNS3 allow for hands-on experience with IDS deployment. Visualization tools like Splunk and Wireshark help analyze network traffic for suspicious activities. Additionally, collaborative platforms enable knowledge sharing, while cloud-based solutions support scalable hybrid IDS models. ICT also aids in research and development, particularly in integrating AI and machine learning for anomaly-based detection, enhancing the effectiveness of IDS systems. Overall, ICT provides a comprehensive framework for studying and implementing various IDS types.

1.3 IDS VS. IPS (INTRUSION PREVENTION SYSTEMS)

The distinction between Intrusion Detection Systems (IDS) and Intrusion Prevention Systems (IPS) is critical in understanding modern cybersecurity strategies. While both serve essential roles in protecting networks from malicious activities, they operate differently regarding threat management.

1.3.1 Intrusion Detection Systems (IDS)

An IDS as given in figure 1.4 is primarily a monitoring tool designed to identify potential security breaches or policy violations within a network or system.

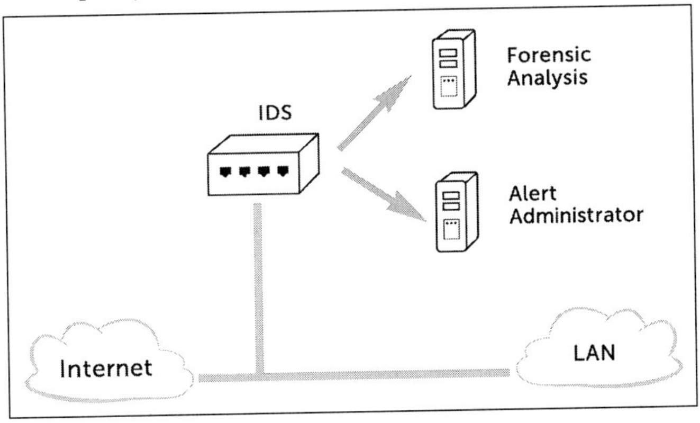

Figure 1.4.: *Intrusion Detection System*

Functionality

- Monitors network traffic or system activities for signs of suspicious behavior.
- Generates alerts when potential intrusions are detected but does not take direct action against them.

Deployment Scenarios

- Often used in environments where real-time intervention is not feasible or necessary.
- Provides valuable insights into network activities that can inform future security measures.

Limitations

- Passive nature means it relies on human intervention for response actions.
- Potential delays in response time can lead to further damage if an intrusion occurs undetected long enough.

1.3.2 Intrusion Prevention Systems (IPS)

In contrast, an IPS as given in figure 1.5 actively prevents intrusions by taking immediate action upon detecting suspicious activity.

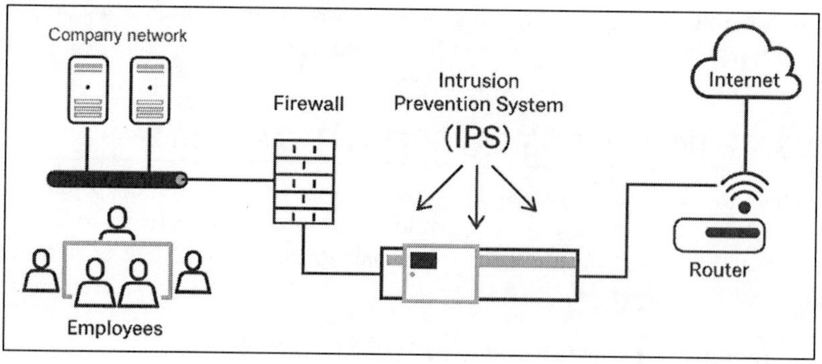

Figure 1.5.: *Intrusion Prevention System*

- **Functionality**: Monitors network traffic similarly to an IDS but is equipped with capabilities to block or mitigate identified threats automatically.
- **Deployment Scenarios**: Commonly integrated into network architectures where proactive security measures are essential. Suitable for high-risk environments where rapid response is necessary to minimize damage from attacks.

Limitations

- May inadvertently block legitimate traffic if not finely tuned, leading to service disruptions.
- Can result in higher operational costs due to increased resource requirements for real-time analysis and decision-making.

Choosing between an IDS and an IPS depends largely on an organization's specific security needs, risk tolerance, and operational capabilities. Many organizations opt for a combination of both systems—using IDS for monitoring and alerting while deploying IPS for active threat prevention—to create a layered security approach that enhances overall resilience against cyber threats.

Video Resources
https://www.perplexity.ai/search/you-tube-link-for-types-of-ids-w uak9aUQNC8uC5m.rk0mw

Use of ICT

Information and Communication Technology (ICT) is integral to the effective implementation and understanding of Intrusion Prevention Systems (IPS). ICT enables real-time monitoring and automated responses to network threats, leveraging tools such as firewalls, anti-malware software, and anomaly detection systems. IPS solutions utilize advanced techniques like signature-based detection, anomaly-based detection, and policy-based detection to identify and block malicious traffic before it causes harm. Through ICT, IPS can analyze network traffic patterns, perform deep packet inspections, and automate threat responses such as dropping suspicious packets or reconfiguring firewalls. Additionally, modern IPS systems integrate artificial intelligence for enhanced threat detection and are often deployed inline within network architectures for proactive security. ICT also supports the scalability of IPS solutions through cloud-based services, ensuring robust protection against evolving cyber threats.

1.4 OVERVIEW OF IDS ARCHITECTURES AND DEPLOYMENT STRATEGIES

The architecture of Intrusion Detection Systems varies based on their deployment locations within an organization's infrastructure. Understanding these architectures is crucial for effective implementation tailored to specific organizational needs.

1.4.1 Host-Based Intrusion Detection Systems (HIDS)

HIDS as given in figure 1.6 operates on individual hosts or devices within a network.

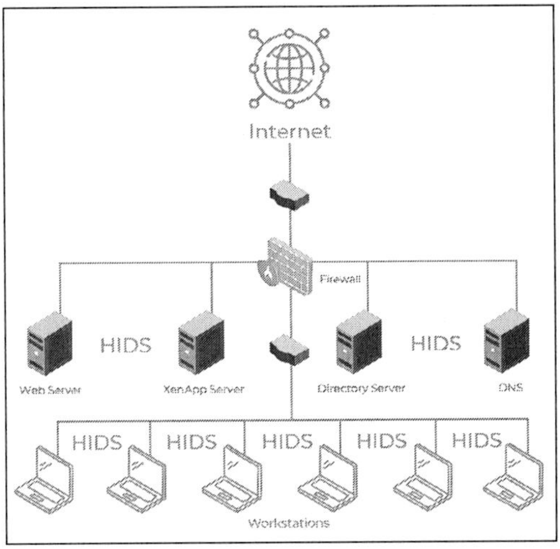

Figure 1.6.: Host Based Intrusion Detection System

- **Architecture:** Installed directly on servers or endpoints, monitoring local logs, file integrity, system calls, and application behavior.

- **Deployment Strategies**: Ideal for environments where sensitive data resides on specific devices requiring close monitoring. Frequently used alongside other security measures such as antivirus software or firewalls for comprehensive protection.
- **Advantages**: Provides detailed insights into host-level activities that may indicate intrusions.
- **Limitations**: Limited visibility across the entire network; does not monitor traffic between devices effectively.

1.4.2 Network-Based Intrusion Detection Systems (NIDS)

NIDS as shown in figure 1.7 monitors network traffic across segments or entire networks.

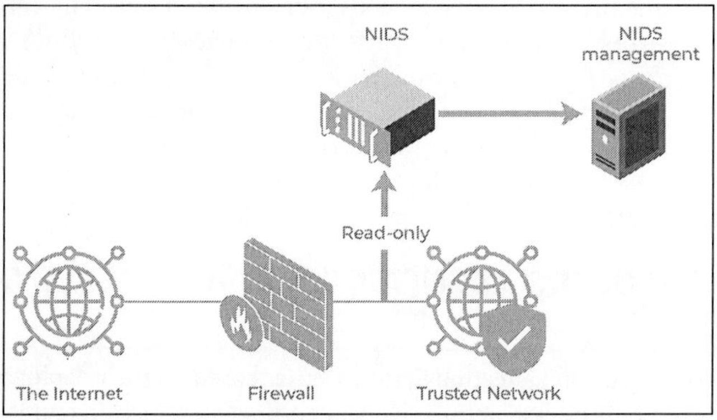

***Figure 1.7.:** Network Based Intrusion Detection System*

- **Architecture**: Deployed at strategic points within the network infrastructure—such as gateways or routers—to analyze incoming and outgoing traffic patterns.
- **Deployment Strategies**: Suitable for organizations with extensive networks requiring visibility into overall traffic behaviors.
- **Advantages:** Offers broad coverage across multiple devices without needing installation on each endpoint.
- **Limitations**: May struggle with encrypted traffic analysis unless configured with decryption capabilities.

1.4.3 Hybrid Deployment Strategies

Many organizations adopt hybrid deployment strategies that combine both HIDS and NIDS.

- **Architecture:** Integrates host-level monitoring with network-level surveillance, creating a comprehensive view of security events across the environment.
- **Deployment Strategies**: Allows organizations to tailor their approach based on specific risks associated with different assets—monitoring critical servers closely while maintaining broader visibility across networks.

Selecting the appropriate architecture and deployment strategy for an IDS requires careful consideration of organizational needs, risk profiles, and existing infrastructure. A well-designed IDS architecture enhances overall security posture by providing timely insights into potential threats while facilitating effective incident response mechanisms. Table 1 gives the difference between HIDS and NIDS.

Table 1.1: Differences between HIDS and NIDS

Categories	HIDS	NIDS
Definition	Host Intrusion Detection System	Network Intrusion Detection System
Type	It doesn't work in real-time	Operates in real-time
Concern	HIDS is related to just a single system, as the name suggests it is only concerned with the threats related to the Host system/ computer,	NIDS is concerned with the entire network system, NIDS examines the activities and traffic of all the systems in the network.
Installation Point	HIDS can be installed on each and every computer or server i.e., anything that can serve as a host.	NIDS being concerned with the network is installed at places like routers or servers as these are the main intersection points in the network system
Execution Process	HIDS operates by taking the snapshot of the current status of the system and comparing it against some already stored malicious tagged snapshots stored in the database, this clearly shows that there is a delay in its operation and activities	NIDS works in real-time by closely examining the data flow and immediately reporting anything unusual.
Information About Attack	HIDS are more informed about the attacks as they are associated with system files and processes.	As the network is very large making it hard to keep track of the integrating functionalities, they are less informed of the attacks
Ease of Installation	As it needs to be installed on every host, the installation process can be tiresome.	Few installation points make it easier to install NIDS
Response Time	Response time is slow	Fast response time

Video Resources
https://www.perplexity.ai/search/you-tube-link-for-types-of-ids-w_uak9aUQNC8uC5m.rkOmw

Use of ICT

Information and Communication Technology (ICT) plays a vital role in hybrid deployment strategies by providing the tools and infrastructure necessary for integrating different environments, such as public and private clouds, into a cohesive system. ICT enables organizations to leverage cloud computing services for flexible access to data and applications, ensuring scalability and efficiency. Key ICT applications in hybrid deployments include

- **Cloud Management Tools**: ICT facilitates the use of cloud management platforms that provide deep visibility into applications and workloads, allowing for optimization, remediation, and troubleshooting across different cloud services.
- **Automation and Orchestration**: ICT supports automation technologies that streamline the deployment and scaling of applications, enhancing agility and reducing manual errors.

- **Security Solutions**: ICT integrates advanced security measures such as zero-trust architectures, encryption, and continuous monitoring to protect hybrid environments from cyber threats.
- **Data Analytics**: ICT tools help analyze network traffic and system logs to detect anomalies and improve security postures in hybrid setups.

Overall, ICT is essential for managing the complexity of hybrid deployments, ensuring seamless integration, and maintaining robust security across diverse environments.

1.5 METRICS FOR EVALUATING IDS EFFECTIVENESS

Evaluating the effectiveness of an Intrusion Detection System is essential for ensuring its reliability in protecting against cyber threats. Several key metrics provide insights into how well an IDS performs its intended functions

1.5.1 True Positive Rate

The true positive rate as given by equation 1, measures the percentage of actual intrusions correctly identified by the system

$$True\,Positive\,Rate = \frac{True\,Positives}{True\,Positives + False\,Negatives} \quad (1)$$

A high true positive rate indicates that the system effectively detects genuine threats without missing significant incidents.

1.5.2 False Positive Rate

The false positive rate as given in equation 2, assesses how often benign activities are incorrectly flagged as intrusions.

$$False\ Positive\ Rate = \frac{False\,Positives}{False\,Positives + True\,Negatives} \quad (2)$$

Minimizing false positives is crucial since excessive alerts can overwhelm security teams and lead to alert fatigue.

1.5.3 Detection Rate

The detection rate as given in equation 3, represents the proportion of actual attacks detected by the system compared to all attempted attacks.

$$Detection\ Rate = \frac{True\,Positives}{True\,Positives + False\,Negatives} \quad (3)$$

A high detection rate signifies that the system successfully identifies most attempted intrusions within its monitored environment.

1.5.4 Response Time

Response time as given in equation 4, measures how quickly an IDS generates alerts after detecting suspicious activity.

$$Response\ Time = Time\ taken\ from\ detection\ to\ alert\ generation \quad (4)$$

Faster response times enable quicker remediation actions, reducing potential damage from intrusions before they escalate further.

By employing these metrics—true positive rate, false positive rate, detection rate, and response time—organizations can effectively evaluate their IDS's performance. Regular assessments help identify areas needing improvement while ensuring that intrusion detection capabilities align with evolving threat landscapes.

Video Resources
https://www.perplexity.ai/search/you-tube-link-for-types-of-ids-w_uak9aUQNC8uC5m.rk0mw

Use of ICT

Information and Communication Technology (ICT) is essential for evaluating the effectiveness of Intrusion Detection Systems (IDS) through various metrics. ICT enables the collection and analysis of data using tools like machine learning and statistical models to calculate detection rates, false alarm rates, and response times. Advanced techniques, such as Receiver Operating Characteristic (ROC) curves and cost-based analysis, help assess IDS performance under different operational conditions. ICT also supports real-time evaluation by integrating monitoring systems that track metrics like True Positive Rate (TPR), False Positive Rate (FPR), and latency in intrusion detection. Furthermore, simulation environments and benchmarking datasets provided by ICT allow for testing IDS under controlled scenarios to measure accuracy, robustness, and fault tolerance. These capabilities ensure comprehensive evaluation and continuous improvement of IDS solutions in diverse cybersecurity environments.

Solved Problem

Evaluate the effectiveness of an Intrusion Detection System (IDS) deployed in a corporate network that monitors incoming traffic for potential intrusions. The data collected during the testing phase is as given in the table.

Factor	Value
Total number of actual attacks (intrusions attempted)	100
Total number of legitimate traffic instances	1,000
Number of attacks correctly detected by the IDS (True Positives, TP)	80
Number of legitimate traffic incorrectly flagged as attacks (False Positives, FP):	20
Number of attacks missed by the IDS (False Negatives, FN):	20
Total time taken by the IDS to alert on all detected intrusions	400 seconds

Using the tabular data, calculate the following metrics:

1. True Positive Rate (TPR)
2. False Positive Rate (FPR)
3. Detection Rate (DR)
4. Average Response Time per intrusion detected

Solution

1. True Positive Rate (TPR)

   $TPR = TP/TP + FN = 80/80 + 20 = 80/100 = 0.8$ or 80%

2. False Positive Rate (FPR)

   First, calculate True Negatives (TN)

   TN =Total legitimate traffic - FP = 1000 - 20 = 980

   Now calculate FPR

   FPR = FP/ FP + TN =20/20 + 980 = 20/1000 = 0.02 or 2%

3. Detection Rate (DR)

   The Detection Rate is equivalent to the True Positive Rate in this context.

   DR = TPR = 80%

4. Average Response Time per Intrusion Detected

   To calculate the average response time per intrusion detected, divide the total time taken by the number of true positives detected

   Average Response Time = Total Time/No. of Intrusions detected = 400 sec/80 = 5 seconds.

Summary of Results

Metric	Calculated Value
True Positive Rate (TPR)	80%
False Positive Rate (FPR)	2%
Detection Rate (DR)	80%
Average Response Time per Intrusion Detected	5 seconds

Conclusion

The evaluation of the Intrusion Detection System shows that it effectively detects threats with an 80% True Positive Rate and Detection Rate. The False Positive Rate is low at 2%, which helps maintain operational efficiency. Additionally, the Average Response Time per intrusion detected is 5 seconds, indicating that alerts are generated promptly. Overall, these metrics suggest that the IDS performs well but could be further improved by reducing false negatives and enhancing detection capabilities.

1.6 CASE STUDY: EVOLUTION AND DEPLOYMENT OF INTRUSION DETECTION SYSTEMS (IDS) IN AN ENTERPRISE NETWORK

The evolution of intrusion detection systems within enterprise networks reflects broader trends in cybersecurity practices over recent decades. As organizations increasingly rely on digital infrastructures, they have recognized the necessity of implementing robust intrusion detection solutions tailored to their unique operational contexts.

1.6.1 Historical Context

In early implementations during the late '90s and early '00s, enterprises primarily utilized signature-based systems due to their effectiveness against known threats prevalent at that time. However, as cybercriminals developed more sophisticated attack vectors—including zero-day exploits—organizations began seeking more adaptive solutions capable of identifying previously unknown threats through anomaly detection techniques.

1.6.2 Current Deployment Strategies

Today's enterprise networks often employ hybrid models combining both HIDS and NIDS approaches.

- **Integration with Existing Infrastructure:** Organizations integrate intrusion detection Capabilities within existing IT frameworks alongside firewalls, SIEM solutions, endpoint protection platforms (EPP), etc., creating layered defenses against diverse attack vectors.
- **Cloud-Based Solutions:** As enterprises migrate toward cloud computing environments, cloud-native intrusion detection solutions have emerged—allowing organizations greater flexibility while maintaining visibility over hybrid cloud architectures without compromising performance or scalability concerns.
- **Machine Learning Enhancements:** Modern enterprise deployments leverage machine learning algorithms capable of analyzing vast amounts of data generated daily—enabling rapid identification patterns indicative of potential intrusions while minimizing manual intervention requirements through automation tools like Security Orchestration Automation Response (SOAR).
- **Continuous Monitoring:** Continuous monitoring practices ensure real-time visibility into all aspects surrounding user behaviors across endpoints—facilitating proactive identification/remediation actions before incidents escalate further down critical paths impacting business operations adversely.

The evolution from basic signature-based systems towards sophisticated hybrid models illustrates how enterprises have adapted their approaches toward intrusion detection over time—reflecting shifts within broader cybersecurity paradigms driven by technological advancements alongside changing threat landscapes faced regularly today. By adopting comprehensive strategies encompassing various deployment methodologies tailored specifically towards organizational needs & risk profiles; businesses can enhance resilience against ever-evolving cyber threats effectively while safeguarding critical assets efficiently moving forward into future challenges ahead.

Video Resources
https://www.perplexity.ai/search/you-tube-link-for-types-of-ids-w_uak9aUQNC8uC5m.rk0mw

Use of ICT

Information and Communication Technology (ICT) plays a critical role in the evolution and deployment of Intrusion Detection Systems (IDS) within enterprise networks. ICT enables the integration of advanced technologies such as machine learning, artificial intelligence, and big data analytics to enhance the detection of both known and unknown threats. Tools like Security Information and Event Management (SIEM) systems aggregate and analyze data from multiple sources, providing real-time monitoring and alerting capabilities. ICT also supports the deployment of IDS in hybrid environments, including on-premises, cloud-based, or edge computing setups, ensuring scalability and adaptability.

Additionally, ICT facilitates the automation of threat detection through signature-based and anomaly-based methods, improving response times and reducing manual intervention. By leveraging ICT, enterprises can implement robust IDS solutions that evolve with emerging threats while maintaining compliance with security standards and regulations.

SUMMARY

- **History and Evolution of IDS**: IDS originated in the 1980s with foundational concepts by James P. Anderson and Dorothy Denning's IDES prototype, leading to commercial systems like Cisco's Netranger and ISS RealSecure.
- **Types of IDS**: IDS systems are categorized into signature-based (detecting known threats), anomaly-based (identifying unusual behavior), and hybrid models (combining both approaches).
- **IDS vs. IPS**: IDS is a passive monitoring system, while IPS is an active system that blocks threats in real-time, operating inline with network traffic.
- **IDS Architectures**: IDS architectures include network-based IDS (NIDS) for monitoring network traffic and host-based IDS (HIDS) for monitoring individual hosts.
- **Deployment Strategies**: Deployment strategies involve placing NIDS at network perimeters and HIDS on critical systems to achieve layered security.
- **Evaluating IDS Effectiveness**: IDS effectiveness is evaluated using metrics like detection accuracy, false-positive rates, and adaptability to new threats, with case studies highlighting enterprise deployments and adaptations to evolving cyber threats.

EXERCISES

A. Subjective Questions

Category-I *(Revised Bloom's Levels-1, 2 & 3: Remember, Understand, Apply)*

1. Define Intrusion Detection Systems (IDS) and explain their purpose in network security.
2. Describe the historical evolution of IDS, highlighting key milestones such as James P. Anderson's report and Dorothy Denning's IDES prototype.
3. Compare and contrast the types of IDS: signature-based, anomaly-based, and hybrid systems.
4. Explain the difference between IDS and IPS with examples of their applications.
5. Discuss the deployment strategies for IDS in enterprise networks, including network-based and host-based systems.

Category-II *(Revised Bloom's Levels 4, 5 & 6: Analyze, Evaluate, Create)*

1. Analyze the advantages and limitations of anomaly-based IDS compared to signature-based IDS in detecting zero-day attacks.
2. Evaluate the effectiveness of IDS using metrics like detection accuracy, false-positive rates, and scalability in high-speed networks.
3. Design a layered security strategy for deploying IDS in an enterprise network, incorporating both NIDS and HIDS.
4. Propose improvements to hybrid IDS systems to address modern threats such as polymorphic malware and advanced persistent threats (APTs).

5. Critically assess a case study where IDS was deployed in an enterprise network to mitigate evolving cyber threats.

B. Objective Questions

Category-I (Revised Bloom's Levels-1, 2 & 3: Remember, Understand, Apply)

1. What is the primary function of an Intrusion Detection System (IDS)?
   (a) Prevent intrusions (b) Detect intrusions
   (c) Encrypt data (d) Monitor user activity
2. Which type of IDS relies on predefined attack patterns for detection?
   (a) Anomaly-based (b) Signature-based
   (c) Hybrid (d) Behavioral-based
3. What distinguishes IPS from IDS?
   (a) IPS blocks threats; IDS monitors and alerts.
   (b) IPS monitors traffic; IDS blocks threats.
   (c) IPS is passive; IDS is active.
   (d) Both perform identical functions.
4. Where is a network-based IDS typically deployed?
   (a) On individual hosts (b) At network perimeters
   (c) In cloud environments (d) On user devices
5. What metric is used to evaluate the accuracy of an IDS?
   (a) CPU consumption (b) False-positive rate
   (c) Detection rate (d) Scalability

Ans.: 1. (b), 2. (b), 3. (a), 4. (b), 5 (b)

Category-II (Revised Bloom's Levels-4, 5 & 6: Analyze, Evaluate, Create)

1. Which type of IDS is most effective for detecting unknown attacks but has a higher false-positive rate?
   (a) Signature-based IDS (b) Anomaly-based IDS
   (c) Hybrid IDS (d) Host-based IDS
2. What is the main drawback of signature-based IDS?
   (a) High computational cost
   (b) Inability to detect new attacks
   (c) Low detection accuracy for known threats
   (d) Excessive false positives
3. Which deployment strategy ensures layered security using both NIDS and HIDS?
   (a) Centralized architecture (b) Distributed architecture
   (c) Perimeter-only protection (d) Tiered infrastructure protection

4. How can hybrid IDS systems be improved to address polymorphic malware threats?
   (a) By increasing signature database size.
   (b) By integrating AI-driven anomaly detection methods.
   (c) By reducing false-positive rates manually.
   (d) By deploying only host-based sensors.
5. Which metric assesses the scalability of an IDS in high-speed networks?
   (a) Detection ate (b) CPU consumption
   (c) False-negative rate (d) Precision

Ans.: 1. (b), 2. (b), 3. (d), 4. (b), 5 (b)

TEACHER'S KNOW MORE

Intrusion Detection Systems (IDS) have evolved significantly since their inception in the 1980s, starting with James P. Anderson's foundational concepts and Dorothy Denning's IDES prototype. IDS systems are categorized into signature-based, anomaly-based, and hybrid models, each offering unique detection capabilities. Signature-based IDS detects known threats, while anomaly-based systems identify unusual behavior, and hybrid systems combine both approaches. IDS differs from Intrusion Prevention Systems (IPS) in that IDS is passive, monitoring and alerting, whereas IPS actively blocks threats in real-time. IDS architectures include network-based and host-based systems, with deployment strategies focusing on layered security by placing NIDS at network perimeters and HIDS on critical hosts. Key metrics for evaluating IDS effectiveness include detection accuracy, false-positive rates, and scalability in high-speed networks. Case studies highlight how enterprises deploy IDS to adapt to evolving cyber threats, integrating advanced features like sandboxing and anomaly detection to enhance network security.

Machine Learning and Arificial Intelligence in IDS

2

UNIT

RATIONALE

This book chapter on **Machine Learning and Artificial Intelligence in IDS** provides a critical foundation for understanding modern cybersecurity challenges and AI-driven solutions by systematically exploring the evolution from traditional rule-based detection to advanced ML and deep learning techniques. It addresses the growing complexity of network threats, emphasizing how machine learning models like Isolation Forests, LOF, and autoencoders enable robust anomaly detection in dynamic environments, while deep learning architectures (e.g., CNNs, LSTMs) enhance intrusion detection in high-dimensional IoT and 5G networks through adaptive pattern recognition. The chapter underscores the importance of **feature engineering** and dataset preparation, detailing methods like BQABC algorithms and density-based clustering to optimize IDS performance by addressing imbalanced data and reducing computational overhead. A comparative analysis highlights the limitations of traditional signature-based IDS against ML-based approaches, which leverage ICT infrastructure for real-time processing, scalability, and adaptive learning, while case studies on AI-enabled IDS in modern networks illustrate practical implementations, such as detecting zero-day exploits and DDoS attacks in cloud and edge environments. By integrating theoretical frameworks with real-world applications, the chapter equips readers to evaluate and deploy AI-driven IDS solutions, balancing accuracy, efficiency, and interpretability in evolving cyber-physical systems.

OUTCOMES

- Understand the role of machine learning models for anomaly detection in identifying deviations from normal network behavior.
- Explore deep learning approaches in IDS, such as CNNs and LSTMs, for enhanced intrusion detection.
- Gain insights into feature engineering and dataset preparation for IDS to optimize model performance.
- Compare ML-based IDS with traditional approaches to highlight their respective strengths and limitations.
- Analyze case studies of AI-enabled IDS in modern networks to demonstrate real-world applications and effectiveness.

2.1 MACHINE LEARNING MODELS FOR ANOMALY DETECTION

Anomaly detection is a critical task in data analysis, aimed at identifying rare items, events, or observations that deviate significantly from the majority of the data. Anomaly detection refers to the identification of patterns in data that do not conform to expected behavior . These anomalies can indicate critical incidents, such as fraud, network intrusions, or system failures. Machine learning (ML) has become a powerful tool for automating anomaly detection processes, leveraging various algorithms to classify data points into normal and anomalous categories.. In the context of cybersecurity, it plays a crucial role in identifying potential intrusions or malicious activities within a network.

2.1.1 Types of Anomaly Detection

Anomaly detection can be categorized into three primary types.

- **Point Anomalies:** A single observation that is significantly different from the rest of the dataset.
- **Contextual Anomalies:** An observation that is considered anomalous only in a specific context (e.g., seasonal effects).
- **Collective Anomalies:** A set of observations that collectively deviate from the expected pattern.

2.1.2 Machine Learning Approaches for Anomaly Detection

Supervised Learning

Supervised anomaly detection requires labeled datasets where instances are marked as normal or anomalous. Common algorithms include:

✓ **Support Vector Machines (SVM):** Effective for binary classification tasks, SVM can identify anomalies by finding a hyperplane that separates normal data points from outliers.

✓ **Neural Networks:** Models like feed forward neural networks can be trained on labeled data to classify instances.

Unsupervised Learning

Unsupervised methods do not require labeled data and are useful when anomalies are not previously known. Techniques include:

✓ **K-Means Clustering:** Groups data points into clusters; points far from any cluster centroid are flagged as anomalies.

✓ **Isolation Forest:** Constructs decision trees to isolate anomalies based on their attributes.

Semi-supervised Learning

This approach combines both labeled and unlabeled data, allowing models to learn from a smaller set of labeled instances while generalizing to unlabeled data.

Example: K-Means Clustering for Anomaly Detection

K-Means clustering is a popular unsupervised learning algorithm used for anomaly detection. It partitions the dataset into K clusters and identifies outliers based on their distance from the nearest cluster center.

Sample Python Program Using K-Means Clustering

```
import numpy as np
import matplotlib.pyplot as plt
```

```
from sklearn.cluster import KMeans
# Generate synthetic dataset
np.random.seed(0)
normal_data = np.random.normal(loc=0, scale=1, size=(100, 2))  # Normal data
anomalous_data = np.random.uniform(low=-6, high=6, size=(10, 2))  # Anomalous data
data = np.vstack((normal_data, anomalous_data))
# Apply K-Means Clustering
kmeans = KMeans(n_clusters=3)
kmeans.fit(data)
labels = kmeans.labels_
# Identify anomalies (points assigned to clusters with fewer members)
unique_labels, counts = np.unique(labels, return_counts=True)
anomaly_labels = unique_labels[counts < 15]  # Threshold for anomaly detection
anomalies = data[np.isin(labels, anomaly_labels)]
# Plotting results
plt.scatter(data[:, 0], data[:, 1], c='blue', label = 'Normal Data', alpha = 0.5)
plt.scatter(anomalies[:, 0], anomalies[:, 1], c = 'red', label = 'Anomalies', marker = 'x')
plt.title('K-Means Clustering for Anomaly Detection')
plt.xlabel('Feature 1')
plt.ylabel('Feature 2')
plt.legend()
plt.show()
```

Explanation of the Code

- **Data Generation:** A synthetic dataset is created with normal data points sampled from a normal distribution and anomalous points sampled uniformly from a larger range.
- **K-Means Clustering:** The KMeans class from sklearn.cluster is used to fit the model on the dataset with n_clusters=3.The fit method trains the model and assigns cluster labels to each point.
- **Anomaly Identification:** Unique labels and their counts are determined. Any cluster with fewer than a specified threshold (e.g., less than 15 members) indicates potential anomalies.
- **Plotting:** The results are visualized using matplotlib, where normal data points are shown in blue and detected anomalies in red.

Expected Output

The scatter plot should visually represent the distribution of normal and anomalous data points. The normal data will appear clustered around the center of the plot, while the anomalies will be scattered away from these clusters.

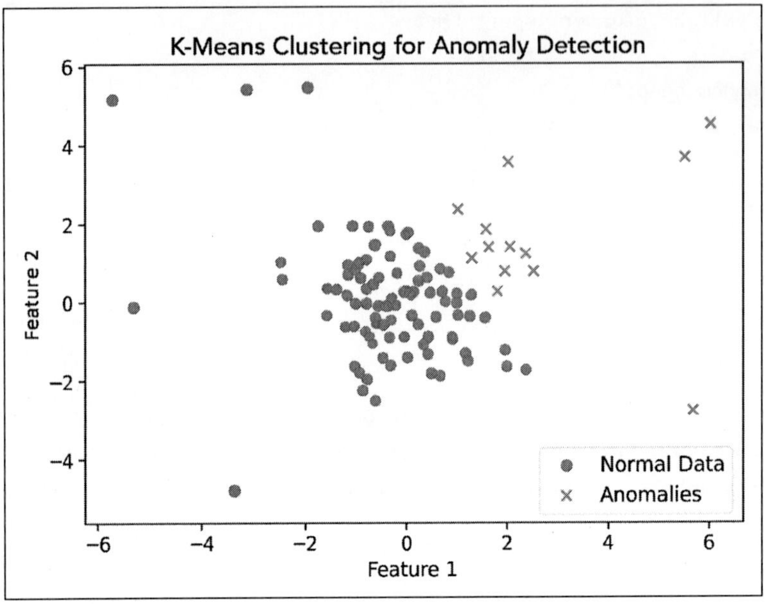

Figure 2.1.: *Output for K-Means Clustering for Anomaly Detection*

Output Description

When the above code is executed, it generates a scatter plot displaying normal data points clustered together in blue and outliers marked in red. The visual representation allows for easy identification of anomalous behavior within the dataset.

Machine learning models for anomaly detection provide powerful tools for identifying unusual patterns in data across various domains. Techniques such as K-Means clustering enable automated detection of anomalies without requiring extensive labeling efforts. By leveraging these models, organizations can enhance their ability to respond to potential threats effectively and maintain high-quality data integrity.

When you run the code, a scatter plot will be displayed showing

Normal data points (in blue) clustered together.

Anomalous points (in red) marked with an 'x'.

Video Resources
https://www.youtube.com/watch?v=OS9xRGKfx4E

Use of ICT

The use of Information and Communication Technology (ICT) in machine learning models for anomaly detection is pivotal for efficient data processing, model training, and real-time anomaly identification. ICT facilitates the collection of large-scale data from diverse sources such as IoT devices, network logs, financial transactions, and healthcare systems, which serves as the foundation for training machine learning models. Real-time data processing is enabled through ICT systems, integrating machine learning algorithms into platforms like cloud services or edge devices, which is critical for applications like fraud detection, cybersecurity, and industrial monitoring. ICT infrastructure, such as GPUs and distributed computing systems, accelerates the training of complex models like neural networks and Isolation Forests. Additionally, cloud-based ICT platforms allow scalable deployment of anomaly detection models, supporting continuous learning by updating models with new data. ICT tools also provide visualization interfaces that help stakeholders interpret detected anomalies, enabling informed decision-making across various domains including finance, healthcare, cybersecurity, and manufacturing.

2.2 DEEP LEARNING APPROACHES IN IDS

Deep learning approaches leverage neural networks to automatically learn and extract intricate patterns from large datasets, enhancing the detection capabilities of IDS.

2.2.1 Key Deep Learning Techniques

Several deep learning architectures have been effectively applied in IDS

- **Convolutional Neural Networks (CNNs):** Primarily used for image data, CNNs are adept at analyzing multidimensional data arrays, making them suitable for detecting anomalies in network traffic patterns.
- **Recurrent Neural Networks (RNNs):** RNNs excel in processing sequential data, which is essential for time-series analysis of network traffic.
- **Long Short-Term Memory (LSTM):** A type of RNN, LSTMs are particularly effective in capturing long-term dependencies in data, enabling them to identify complex attack patterns over time.
- **Deep Belief Networks (DBNs):** These networks are useful for unsupervised learning tasks and can be employed to pre-train models before fine-tuning with labeled data.
- **Autoencoders:** Utilized for anomaly detection by learning to reconstruct normal behavior and flagging deviations as potential intrusions.

2.2.2 Advantages of Deep Learning in IDS

- **High Detection Accuracy:** DL models can achieve superior accuracy due to their ability to learn complex features directly from raw data.
- **Adaptability:** They can continuously learn from new data, making them resilient against evolving threats.
- **Automated Feature Extraction:** Unlike traditional methods that require manual feature selection, DL models autonomously identify relevant features from raw inputs.
- **Scalability:** DL approaches can handle vast amounts of data efficiently, which is crucial given the exponential growth of network traffic.

2.2.3 Challenges

Despite their advantages, deep learning approaches face several challenges

- **Data Requirements:** DL models require large labeled datasets for training, which may not always be available.
- **Computational Resources:** Training deep networks demands significant computational power and time.

- **Interpretability:** The "black box" nature of deep learning models makes it difficult to interpret their decision-making processes.

A simple Python program that demonstrates a basic implementation of an LSTM model for intrusion detection using Keras is given here.

This example assumes that you have preprocessed your dataset and split it into training and testing sets.

```
import numpy as np
from keras.models import Sequential
from keras.layers import LSTM, Dense, Dropout
# Generate dummy dataset
# Assume X_train is shaped (num_samples, timesteps, num_features)
X_train = np.random.rand(1000, 10, 5)  # 1000 samples, 10 timesteps, 5 features
y_train = np.random.randint(0, 2, 1000)  # Binary classification
# Build LSTM model
model = Sequential()
model.add(LSTM(50, return_sequences=True, input_shape=(X_train.shape[1], X_train.shape[2])))
model.add(Dropout(0.2))
model.add(LSTM(50))
model.add(Dropout(0.2))
model.add(Dense(1, activation='sigmoid'))  # Binary output
# Compile model
model.compile(loss='binary_crossentropy', optimizer='adam', metrics=['accuracy'])
# Train model
model.fit(X_train, y_train, epochs=10, batch_size=32)
# Sample output prediction on new data
X_test = np.random.rand(10, 10, 5)  # New test samples
predictions = model.predict(X_test)
print(predictions)
```

The program aims to create a synthetic dataset, build an LSTM model, train it on the dataset, and then use it to make predictions on new data. LSTMs are particularly well-suited for time-series data, making them a good choice for intrusion detection systems that analyze sequences of network traffic.

Step-by-Step Explanation

Importing Libraries

```
import numpy as np
from keras.models import Sequential
from keras.layers import LSTM, Dense, Dropout
```

- **numpy**: A fundamental package for numerical computing in Python. It is used here to generate random datasets.
- **Keras**: A high-level neural networks API that runs on top of TensorFlow. It simplifies the process of building and training deep learning models.

- **Sequential**: A linear stack of layers in Keras. It allows you to build models layer by layer.
- **LSTM, Dense, Dropout**: These are specific types of layers used in the model
- **LSTM**: The core layer that processes sequences.
- **Dense**: A fully connected layer used for output.
- **Dropout**: A regularization technique to prevent overfitting by randomly setting a fraction of input units to 0 during training.

Generating Dummy Dataset

```
X_train = np.random.rand(1000, 10, 5)  # 1000 samples, 10 timesteps, 5 features
Y_train = np.random.randint(0, 2, 1000)  # Binary classification
```

X_train: This creates a random dataset with shape (1000, 10, 5), meaning:

1000 samples: Total number of training examples.

10 timesteps: Each sample contains sequences of length 10 (e.g., representing time).

5 features: Each timestep has 5 features (e.g., different metrics of network traffic).

Building the LSTM Model

```
model = Sequential()
model.add(LSTM(50, return_sequences=True, input_shape=(X_train.shape[1], X_train.shape[2])))
model.add(Dropout(0.2))
model.add(LSTM(50))
model.add(Dropout(0.2))
model.add(Dense(1, activation='sigmoid'))  # Binary output
```

Sequential(): Initializes a sequential model.

- **LSTM Layer**: The first LSTM layer has 50 units and is set to return sequences (return_sequences=True). This means it will output the full sequence of outputs for each input sequence (needed when stacking LSTMs).

  input_shape=(X_train.shape, X_train.shape) specifies the shape of the input data (10 timesteps and 5 features).
- **Dropout Layer**: After each LSTM layer, a Dropout layer is added with a rate of 0.2, meaning that during training, it will randomly set 20% of the inputs to zero to help prevent overfitting.
- **Second LSTM Layer**: Another LSTM layer with 50 units, which processes the output from the previous layer but does not return sequences since it's followed by a dense output layer.
- **Output Layer**: A Dense layer with a single unit and a sigmoid activation function is used for binary classification. The sigmoid function outputs a value between 0 and 1, representing the probability of an intrusion.

Compiling the Model

```
model.compile(loss='binary_crossentropy',optimizer='adam', metrics=['accuracy'])
```

The model is compiled with

loss='binary_crossentropy': This loss function is suitable for binary classification problems.

optimizer='adam': Adam is an adaptive learning rate optimization algorithm that is efficient and widely used.

metrics=['accuracy']: This specifies that we want to track accuracy during training.

Training the Model

```
model.fit(X_train, y_train, epochs=10, batch_size=32)
```

The model is trained using the fit method

X_train and y_train are passed as inputs.

epochs=10: The model will go through the entire dataset ten times.

batch_size=32: The number of samples processed before updating the model's weights.

Making Predictions

```
X_test = np.random.rand(10, 10, 5)  # New test samples
predictions = model.predict(X_test)
print(predictions)
```

X_test: A new synthetic dataset with shape (10, 10, 5) is created for testing purposes.

predictions: The predict method generates predictions for the test samples. Each prediction will be a probability value between 0 and 1 indicating whether an intrusion is likely (closer to 1) or not (closer to 0).

The predictions are printed out.

Output

Epoch 1/10

/usr/local/lib/python3.11/dist-packages/keras/src/layers/rnn/rnn.py:204: UserWarning: Do not pass an `input_shape`/`input_dim` argument to a layer. When using Sequential models, prefer using an `Input(shape)` object as the first layer in the model instead.

super().__init__(**kwargs)

32/32 -------------------------------- 5s 20ms/step - accuracy: 0.5330 - loss: 0.6947

Epoch 2/10

32/32 -------------------------------- 1s 19ms/step - accuracy: 0.4845 - loss: 0.6955

Epoch 3/10

32/32 -------------------------------- 1s 19ms/step - accuracy: 0.5268 - loss: 0.6937

Epoch 4/10

32/32 -------------------------------- 1s 21ms/step - accuracy: 0.5041 - loss: 0.6939

Epoch 5/10

32/32 -------------------------------- 1s 12ms/step - accuracy: 0.5096 - loss: 0.6934

Epoch 6/10

```
32/32 --------------------------------1s 14ms/step - accuracy: 0.4818 - loss: 0.6938
Epoch 7/10
32/32 -------------------------------- 0s 12ms/step - accuracy: 0.5121 - loss: 0.6934
Epoch 8/10
32/32 -------------------------------- 0s 13ms/step - accuracy: 0.5011 - loss: 0.6932
Epoch 9/10
32/32 -------------------------------- 1s 11ms/step - accuracy: 0.5210 - loss: 0.6919
Epoch 10/10
32/32 -------------------------------- 1s 12ms/step - accuracy: 0.4885 - loss: 0.6952
1/1 -------------------------------- 0s 349ms/step
[0.4867174]
[0.4793429]
[0.47522944]
[0.48157278]
[0.4847993]
[0.48962674]
[0.47823346]
[0.49837416]
[0.48476255]
[0.48812813]
```

Video Resources
https://www.youtube.com/watch?v=RuhNpsRZHcU

Use of ICT

The integration of Information and Communication Technology (ICT) with deep learning approaches enhances Intrusion Detection Systems (IDS) by enabling efficient data processing, scalable model deployment, and real-time threat detection. ICT infrastructure supports the collection and preprocessing of large-scale network datasets like CICDDoS2019 and CICIDS-2017, which are critical for training deep learning models such as convolutional neural networks (CNNs), long short-term memory (LSTM) networks, and hybrid architectures (e.g., CNN-LSTM combinations).

For instance, cloud computing and distributed systems accelerate model training, allowing complex architectures to achieve high accuracy (up to 99.76% in IoT-5G environments). ICT also facilitates real-time anomaly detection through edge computing and IoT integration, enabling immediate response to threats like DDoS attacks in cyber-physical systems.

Additionally, data augmentation and balancing techniques, supported by ICT tools, address challenges like imbalanced datasets, improving model robustness in multi-class classification scenarios. Visualization dashboards and automated updates via ICT platforms further ensure continuous adaptation to evolving threats, as seen in hybrid models outperforming traditional methods in dynamic network environments.

2.3 FEATURE ENGINEERING AND DATASET PREPARATION FOR IDS

Feature engineering is a crucial step in developing effective Intrusion Detection Systems (IDS). It involves the selection, transformation, and creation of features from raw data to improve model performance. Proper feature engineering can enhance the accuracy, efficiency, and interpretability of machine learning models used in IDS.

2.3.1 Importance of Feature Engineering

- **Dimensionality Reduction:** Reducing the number of features helps mitigate the curse of dimensionality, leading to faster training times and reduced overfitting.
- **Improved Model Performance:** Well-engineered features can lead to better predictive performance by providing more relevant information to the model.
- **Interpretability:** Selecting meaningful features makes it easier to understand model decisions, which is critical in security applications.

2.3.2 Common Techniques in Feature Engineering

- **Feature Selection:** Identifying and selecting the most relevant features from the dataset.
- **Techniques include:** Filter Methods: Statistical tests to evaluate feature relevance (e.g., chi-square test).
- **Wrapper Methods:** Using a predictive model to evaluate combinations of features.
- **Embedded Methods:** Feature selection occurs during model training (e.g., LASSO regression).
- **Feature Transformation:** Modifying existing features to improve their usefulness.

2.3.3 Techniques

- **Normalization/Standardization**: Scaling features to a common range or distribution.
- **Log Transformation**: Reducing skewness in data distributions.
- **Polynomial Features**: Creating interaction terms or higher-degree features.

2.3.4 Feature Creation

Generating new features based on existing ones.

Examples include:

Time-based features (e.g., time of day, duration).

Aggregated metrics (e.g., average bytes per connection).

2.3.5 Dataset Preparation

Preparing a dataset for IDS involves several steps

- **Data Collection**: Gathering network traffic data from various sources (e.g., logs, packet captures).
- **Data Cleaning**: Removing duplicates, handling missing values, and correcting inconsistencies.

- **Labeling Data**: Assigning labels to data points indicating whether they are normal or represent an intrusion.
- **Splitting Data**: Dividing the dataset into training, validation, and test sets to ensure robust model evaluation.

A Python program that demonstrates basic feature engineering techniques using a synthetic dataset for an IDS scenario is given here.

```
import pandas as pd
import numpy as np
from sklearn.model_selection import train_test_split
from sklearn.preprocessing import StandardScaler
# Generate synthetic dataset
np.random.seed(42)
data_size = 1000
data = {
    'duration': np.random.exponential(scale=10, size=data_size),
# Connection duration
    'src_bytes': np.random.randint(0, 1000, size=data_size),
# Source bytes
    'dst_bytes': np.random.randint(0, 1000, size=data_size),
# Destination bytes
    'label': np.random.choice([0, 1], size=data_size)
# 0 for normal, 1 for intrusion
}
# Create DataFrame
df = pd.DataFrame(data)
# Feature Engineering
# Normalizing the numerical features
scaler = StandardScaler()
df[['duration', 'src_bytes', 'dst_bytes']] = scaler.fit_transform(df
[['duration', 'src_bytes', 'dst_bytes']])
# Splitting the dataset into training and testing sets
X = df.drop('label', axis=1)
y = df['label']
X_train, X_test, y_train, y_test = train_test_split(X, y, test_size=0.2,
random_state=42)
# Output the prepared datasets
print("Training set shape:", X_train.shape)
print("Test set shape:", X_test.shape)
print("\nFirst few rows of the training set:")
print(X_train.head())
```

Output

Training set shape: (800, 3)

Test set shape: (200, 3)

First few rows of the training set:

	duration	src_bytes	dst bytes
29	−0.951564	−1.659175	−1.282471
535	1.979032	−1.417302	1.427283
695	−0.030150	1.417994	−0.253540
557	−0.970451	0.789794	−0.087924
836	1.533694	−1.091444	−1.522085

Feature engineering and dataset preparation are vital components in developing effective IDS solutions. By applying techniques such as feature selection, transformation, and creation while ensuring proper dataset preparation practices, practitioners can significantly enhance the performance of their intrusion detection models. This foundational work enables better detection rates and reduced false positives in real-world applications.

Video Resources
https://www.youtube.com/watch?v=Oii2OsWt1sg

Use of ICT

The use of Information and Communication Technology (ICT) in feature engineering and dataset preparation for Intrusion Detection Systems (IDS) plays a crucial role in enhancing the efficiency and accuracy of machine learning-based cybersecurity solutions. ICT enables the collection and preprocessing of large-scale datasets, such as NSL-KDD, UNSW-NB15, and BoT-IoT, which are essential for training IDS models. Advanced ICT tools support feature selection and construction techniques, such as Binary Quantum-inspired Artificial Bee Colony (BQABC) algorithms and Genetic Programming, to identify informative features while reducing computational complexity. By leveraging edge computing infrastructure, ICT facilitates real-time data processing close to IoT devices, minimizing latency and improving responsiveness for time-sensitive applications. Additionally, ICT platforms provide robust storage and computational capabilities for handling high-dimensional datasets, ensuring secure communication and efficient model deployment. This integration of ICT with feature engineering methods enhances IDS performance by optimizing the trade-off between accuracy and computational cost while enabling precise classification of network attacks, including zero-day threats.

2.4 COMPARISON OF ML BASED AND TRADITIONAL IDS APPROACHES

Traditional IDS often rely on signature-based detection methods that compare incoming traffic against known threat signatures. While effective for known threats, these systems struggle with novel attacks. In contrast, ML-based IDS can adapt to new threats by learning from data patterns. The comparison between the Traditional and ML based IDS is as given in Table 2.1.

Table 2.1: *Comparison between Traditional and ML based IDS*

Feature	Traditional IDS	ML-Based IDS
Detection Method	Signature Based	Anomaly Detection
Adaptability	Limited	High

Feature	Traditional IDS	ML-Based IDS
False Positive Rate	Higher	Lower
Response Time	Slower	Faster

Video Resources
https://www.youtube.com/watch?v=OS9xRGKfx4E

Use of ICT

The use of Information and Communication Technology (ICT) in comparing machine learning (ML)-based and traditional intrusion detection system (IDS) approaches highlights advancements in cybersecurity. ICT facilitates the deployment of ML-based IDS by enabling the collection and processing of large-scale network traffic data from IoT devices, industrial systems, and cloud environments. Traditional IDS methods, such as signature-based and rule-based systems, rely heavily on predefined patterns and rules, making them less effective against evolving or zero-day attacks. In contrast, ML-based IDS leverages ICT infrastructure to train models on labeled datasets, allowing for dynamic learning and detection of both known and unknown threats. ICT platforms also support advanced ML techniques like federated learning and active learning, which enhance privacy and personalization in IDS for critical infrastructures. Furthermore, deep learning (DL) models, supported by ICT's computational power, offer superior accuracy by identifying complex patterns in high-dimensional data.

However, ML-based approaches require significant computational resources for training and are sensitive to issues like class imbalance and concept drift. By integrating ICT with both traditional and ML-based IDS, organizations can achieve a balance between efficiency, adaptability, and resource optimization to address diverse cybersecurity challenges effectively.

2.5 CASE STUDY: AI-ENABLED IDS IN MODERN NETWORKS

Several organizations have successfully implemented AI-enabled IDS to enhance their cybersecurity posture.

- **Financial Sector**: Banks utilize AI-driven systems to protect sensitive financial transactions from fraud by analyzing transaction patterns and user behaviors.
- **Healthcare**: Hospitals employ AI-based IDS to safeguard patient records against unauthorized access by monitoring network activities for anomalies.
- **Government Networks**: Government agencies leverage AI technologies to secure sensitive information and protect national security interests from cyber threats.

Scenario Based Question

A financial institution has been experiencing unusual network traffic patterns that suggest potential botnet activities. To enhance their security posture, they decide to implement an AI-powered IDS that utilizes machine learning algorithms to analyze network traffic and detect anomalies. How can the financial institution effectively utilize an AI-enabled IDS to detect and mitigate botnet attacks in real-time?

Solution

To address this problem, the institution employs a machine learning model trained on a labeled dataset of network traffic, such as the CSE-CIC-IDS2018 dataset. The model will be designed to identify patterns indicative of botnet behavior.

Implementation Steps

- **Data Collection:** Gather historical network traffic data, including normal and malicious activities.
- **Data Preprocessing:** Clean the data by removing duplicates and handling missing values.
- **Feature Engineering:** Select relevant features that can help distinguish between normal and malicious traffic.
- **Model Training:** Use machine learning algorithms (e.g., Random Forest, Support Vector Machine) to train the model on the prepared dataset.
- **Real-Time Monitoring:** Implement the trained model to analyze incoming traffic and flag potential intrusions.

A simplified Python program that demonstrates how to prepare a dataset, train a Random Forest model, and evaluate its performance in detecting anomalies (botnet attacks) is given here.

```
import pandas as pd
from sklearn.model_selection import train_test_split
from sklearn.ensemble import RandomForestClassifier
from sklearn.metrics import classification_report, confusion_matrix
# Load synthetic dataset (for demonstration purposes)
# Assume we have a CSV file with features and labels
data = {
    'duration': [0.1, 0.2, 0.3, 0.1, 0.5, 0.2],
# Example connection durations
   'src_bytes': [500, 600, 700, 800, 900, 100], # Source bytes transferred
    'dst_bytes': [300, 400, 500, 600, 700, 800],
# Destination bytes transferred
    'label': [0, 1, 1, 0, 1, 0]
# Label: 0 = normal, 1 = botnet attack
}
# Create DataFrame from synthetic data
df = pd.DataFrame(data)
# Split the dataset into features and labels
X = df.drop('label', axis=1)
y = df['label']
# Split into training and testing sets
X_train, X_test, y_train, y_test = train_test_split(X, y, test_size=0.33, 
random_state=42)
# Initialize and train the Random Forest Classifier
model = RandomForestClassifier(n_estimators=100)
model.fit(X_train, y_train)
```

```
# Make predictions on the test set
y_pred = model.predict(X_test)
# Evaluate the model’s performance
print(“Confusion Matrix:”)
print(confusion_matrix(y_test, y_pred))
print(“\nClassification Report:”)
print(classification_report(y_test, y_pred))
```

When you run this program,

- **Confusion Matrix:** Displays true positives (TP), true negatives (TN), false positives (FP), and false negatives (FN) for evaluating model performance.
- **Classification Report**: Provides precision, recall, F1-score for each class (normal vs. botnet attack).

Output

```
Confusion Matrix:
           Predicted
              0   1
Actual      0 [1   0]|
            1 [1   0]

Classification Report:
               precision    recall  f1-score   support

           0       0.50      1.00      0.67         1
           1       0.00      0.00      0.00         1

    accuracy                           0.50         2
   macro avg       0.25      0.50      0.33         2
weighted avg       0.25      0.50      0.33         2
```

To calculate the accuracy of the model from the provided program, you can derive it from the confusion matrix or directly using the accuracy_score function from sklearn. metrics.

Accuracy as given in equation 1 is defined the ratio of correctly predicted observations to the total observations. It can be calculated using the formula

$$Accuracy = \frac{TP + TN}{TP + TN + FP + FN} \tag{1}$$

Where,

TP (True Positive): Correctly predicted positive cases (botnet attacks).

TN (True Negative): Correctly predicted negative cases (normal traffic).

FP (False Positive): Incorrectly predicted positive cases.

FN (False Negative): Incorrectly predicted negative cases.

Step by Step Calculation

1. Identify the values from the confusion matrix

   TP = 0 ,TN = 1, FP = 0, FN = 1

2. Plug these values into the accuracy formula

$$\text{Accuracy} = \frac{TP + TN}{TP + TN + FP + FN} = \frac{0+1}{0+1+0+1} = \frac{1}{2} = 0.5$$

3. Convert to Percentage

Accuracy = 0.5 x 100 = 50 %

The accuracy of the model based on the provided confusion matrix values is 50%. This means that half of the predictions made by the model were correct. The implementation of an AI-enabled IDS in a banking environment demonstrates how machine learning can effectively detect botnet attacks through real-time analysis of network traffic patterns. By utilizing techniques such as feature engineering and model training with historical data, organizations can significantly enhance their security measures against evolving cyber threats. This case study illustrates not only the process of developing an AI-powered IDS but also highlights its practical application in safeguarding critical infrastructure within modern networks.

The integration of machine learning and artificial intelligence into Intrusion Detection Systems marks a significant advancement in cybersecurity. These technologies not only enhance the detection capabilities of IDS but also enable organizations to respond proactively to evolving cyber threats. As cyber-attacks become more sophisticated, investing in AI-powered IDS is essential for maintaining robust security measures across various industries.

Video Resources
https://www.youtube.com/watch?v=tKJlGScpfbw

Use of ICT

The use of Information and Communication Technology (ICT) in AI-enabled Intrusion Detection Systems (IDS) for modern networks is transformative, providing advanced tools and infrastructure for detecting and mitigating cyber threats. ICT facilitates the collection, processing, and analysis of vast amounts of network traffic data from IoT devices, cloud systems, and high-density communication networks. AI-driven IDS, supported by ICT, leverages machine learning (ML) and deep learning (DL) algorithms to identify known and unknown threats, such as zero-day attacks, by analyzing patterns and anomalies in real-time. ICT also enables the deployment of scalable AI models across diverse environments, including edge computing systems, ensuring low-latency responses to potential intrusions. Moreover, ICT tools automate repetitive tasks like monitoring network logs and generating alerts, freeing up security analysts to focus on complex investigations. AI-powered IDS systems can adapt to evolving threats by continuously learning from new data, a capability supported by robust ICT infrastructure. For instance, combining ML models like CNNs and LSTMs with ICT resources has shown high accuracy in detecting malicious activities in network traffic.

Additionally, ICT enhances the scalability and flexibility of IDS solutions, making them suitable for modern dynamic networks while ensuring compliance with stringent data privacy regulations. Overall, the integration of ICT with AI-enabled IDS strengthens cybersecurity by enabling real-time threat detection, automated responses, and proactive defense mechanisms.

SUMMARY

- **Machine Learning Models for Anomaly Detection**: Identify deviations from normal network behavior.
- **Deep Learning Approaches in IDS**: Enhance detection accuracy with complex pattern analysis.
- **Feature Engineering and Dataset Preparation**: Critical for optimizing ML/DL models.
- **Comparison of ML-Based and Traditional IDS Approaches**: ML-based systems detect unknown threats more effectively.
- **Case Studies: AI-Enabled IDS in Modern Networks**: Demonstrate superior performance in real-world applications.

EXERCISES

A. Subjective Questions

Category-I (Revised Bloom's Levels-1, 2 & 3)

1. Define anomaly detection and explain its importance in Intrusion Detection Systems (IDS).
2. Describe the role of machine learning models in detecting anomalies within network traffic.
3. Explain the difference between supervised and unsupervised learning approaches in anomaly detection.
4. List the key steps involved in feature engineering and dataset preparation for IDS.
5. Compare traditional IDS approaches with ML-based IDS in terms of efficiency and adaptability.

Category-II (Revised Bloom's Levels-4, 5 & 6)

1. Analyze the advantages and limitations of deep learning models like CNNs or RNNs in IDS applications.
2. Design a workflow for preparing a dataset and selecting features for training an ML model for anomaly detection in IDS.
3. Evaluate the effectiveness of AI-enabled IDS in modern networks using a real-world case study example.
4. Propose improvements to an existing ML-based IDS by integrating advanced feature selection techniques or hybrid models.
5. Critically assess the scalability of ML-based IDS compared to traditional systems in large-scale enterprise environments.

B. Objective Questions

Category-I (Revised Bloom's Levels-1, 2 & 3)

1. What is the primary goal of machine learning models in anomaly detection?

(a) Predicting future attacks
(b) Detecting deviations from normal behavior
(c) Generating attack signatures
(d) Encrypting network data

2. Which dataset is commonly used for evaluating IDS performance?
(a) CIFAR-10 (b) NSL-KDD
(c) ImageNet (d) MNIST

3. Which algorithm is density-based and commonly used for unsupervised anomaly detection?
(a) K-means (b) DBSCAN
(c) SVM (d) Random Forest

4. What is the main limitation of traditional IDS compared to ML-based IDS?
(a) High computational cost (b) Inability to detect unknown threats
(c) Complex implementation process (d) Lack of scalability

5. What is an example of unsupervised learning for anomaly detection?
(a) Logistic Regression (b) Autoencoders
(c) Decision Trees (d) Naive Bayes

Ans.: 1. (b), 2. (b), 3. (b), 4. (b), 5. (b)

Category-II (Revised Bloom's Levels-4, 5 & 6)

1. Which deep learning model would you recommend for detecting temporal anomalies in network traffic, and why? *(Open-ended MCQ with justification)*

2. Identify the most suitable feature engineering technique for handling imbalanced datasets in IDS applications:
(a) Principal Component Analysis (PCA)
(b) SMOTE (Synthetic Minority Oversampling Technique)
(c) One-Hot Encoding
(d) Bag-of-Words

3. Which scenario demonstrates the effectiveness of AI-enabled IDS in modern networks?
(a) Detecting malware using static signatures
(b) Identifying zero-day attacks through pattern recognition
(c) Blocking IP addresses based on predefined rules
(d) Scanning emails for known phishing links

4. What is a key challenge when deploying deep learning models for anomaly detection in real-time systems?
(a) Lack of labeled datasets
(b) High computational requirements
(c) Limited accuracy on small datasets
(d) Inability to process unstructured data

5. How can hybrid models improve the performance of ML-based IDS? *(Open-ended MCQ with justification)*

Ans.: 1. (b), 2. (b), 3. (b), 4. (b), 5. (b)

TEACHER'S KNOW MORE

To enhance teaching effectiveness for the topics covered in this unit, educators can delve deeper into the nuances of machine learning models for anomaly detection, such as Random Forest and SVM, which are evaluated using datasets like CICIDS-2017. Deep learning approaches, including CNNs and RNNs, are particularly effective in handling complex data patterns, with studies highlighting their role in improving IDS accuracy. Proper dataset preprocessing and feature engineering techniques like SMOTE and PCA are crucial for optimizing model performance. When comparing ML-based and traditional IDS approaches, educators can emphasize how ML-based systems adaptively detect unknown threats, reducing false positives but requiring more computational resources. Case studies on AI-enabled IDS in modern networks, such as IoT environments and enterprise systems, demonstrate their effectiveness in combating evolving cyber threats. By integrating these insights, educators can design engaging lectures and practical demonstrations that highlight real-world applications of ML/AI in IDS while addressing challenges like dataset preparation and computational complexity.

Intentionally Left Blank!

IDS for Emerging Technologies

3

UNIT

RATIONALE

This chapter explores the integration of Intrusion Detection Systems (IDS) with emerging technologies, addressing the unique challenges and opportunities they present. It begins with IoT-based IDS, which tackle the resource constraints and dynamic environments of IoT networks, followed by cloud-based IDS that focus on overcoming scalability and latency issues in distributed systems. The chapter delves into blockchain networks, highlighting how blockchain's decentralized and immutable nature enhances IDS capabilities in securing peer-to-peer transactions. Mobile and wireless network IDS are discussed in the context of their vulnerability to dynamic threats and resource limitations, with emphasis on lightweight IDS solutions for constrained environments. Finally, a case study on "Securing Emerging Technologies at GlobalTech Innovations" illustrates practical applications and trends, showcasing how AI-driven IDS solutions are tailored to protect cutting-edge technologies against sophisticated cyber threats.

OUTCOMES

- **Understand IoT Intrusion Detection Systems**: Students will be able to design and implement IDS solutions tailored for IoT environments, addressing unique challenges such as resource constraints and dynamic network conditions.
- **Analyze Cloud-Based IDS Challenges and Solutions**: Students will analyze the scalability and latency challenges in cloud-based IDS and propose effective solutions to enhance detection accuracy and efficiency.
- **Apply IDS in Blockchain Networks**: Students will understand how IDS can be integrated into blockchain networks to enhance security and transparency, leveraging blockchain's decentralized nature.
- **Develop IDS for Mobile and Wireless Networks**: Students will design IDS solutions for mobile and wireless networks, focusing on lightweight approaches to address resource limitations and dynamic threats.
- **Evaluate Trends in Lightweight IDS**: Students will evaluate the effectiveness of lightweight IDS solutions in resource-constrained environments and propose strategies for optimizing their performance in emerging technologies.

Emerging technologies are changing the landscape of cybersecurity, requiring more sophisticated and adaptive intrusion detection systems (IDS). Traditional IDS have limitations, making it necessary to enhance their capabilities with artificial intelligence (AI). Autonomous Intrusion Detection Systems (AIDS) represent a significant advancement in cybersecurity, aimed at identifying and mitigating unauthorized activities within networks without human intervention. These systems continuously monitor, analyze, and respond to potential security threats in real time1. The fundamental concept behind AIDS is to automate the detection process, reducing the time taken to identify breaches and minimizing the need for manual monitoring. This automation is achieved through advanced algorithms and machine learning techniques that enable the systems to learn from historical data and adapt to new threats.

3.1 IOT INTRUSION DETECTION SYSTEMS

The Internet of Things (IoT) is rapidly expanding, with predictions estimating 41.6 billion connected devices by 2025. This growth introduces significant security challenges, making IoT networks prime targets for cyberattacks. Traditional security measures like firewalls and antivirus software are often insufficient to protect diverse IoT infrastructures, highlighting the need for Intrusion Detection Systems (IDS). The IOT based Intrusion Detection System is as shown in figure 3.1.

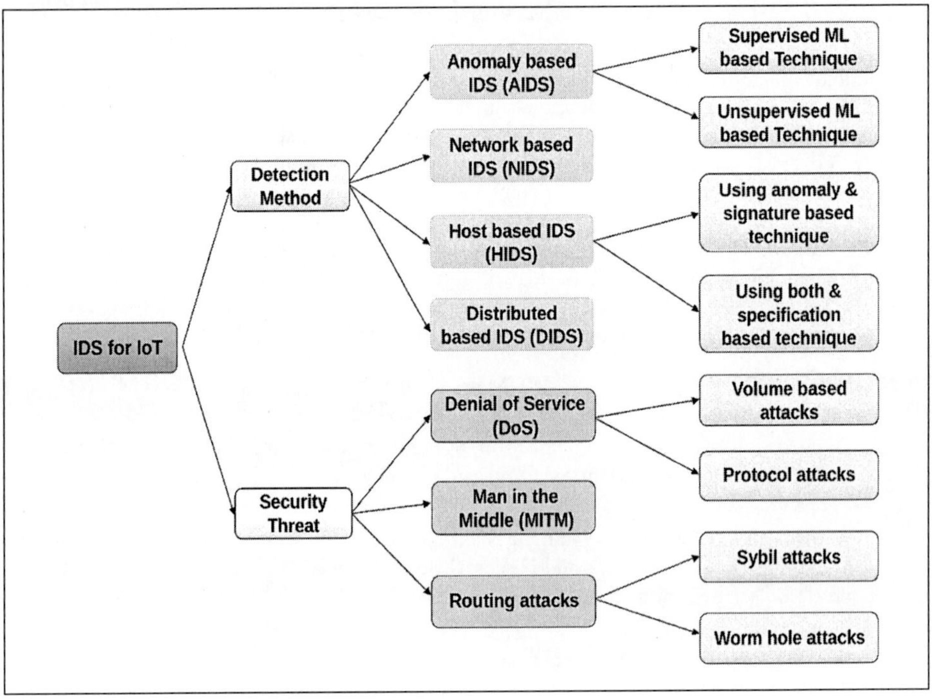

Figure 3.1.: *IOT Intrusion Detection System*

3.1.1 What is an Intrusion Detection System (IDS)?

An IDS is a system that monitors network traffic and system activities for malicious or suspicious behavior. It identifies potential security breaches and reports them to administrators, providing crucial information such as the source and target addresses of the intrusion, and the type of attack1. Unlike firewalls, which prevent unauthorized access, IDS detect intrusions that have already bypassed initial security measures.

3.1.2 Types of Intrusion Detection Systems

- **Network Intrusion Detection System (NIDS):** NIDS monitors network traffic at strategic points to detect and analyze suspicious packets. NIDS can be either hardware or software-based and can be attached to various network mediums.

- **Host Intrusion Detection System (HIDS):** HIDS operates on individual devices, monitoring traffic entering and exiting the device to detect intrusions. Host-based sensors are installed on the host machine to detect possible attacks1. HIDS can obtain data from system logs, OS processes logs, and contents of objects not reflected in standard OS audit and logging mechanisms.
- **Hybrid IDS:** This approach combines NIDS and HIDS to leverage the advantages of both, enhancing overall intrusion detection performance. However, hybrid IDS can be more complex and expensive to manage.

3.1.3 Detection Methods

- **Signature-Based IDS**: This method uses a database of known attack signatures to identify malicious activities. It is effective against known threats but struggles with new or modified attacks.
- **Anomaly-Based IDS**: Anomaly-based IDS establishes a baseline of normal network activity and identifies deviations from this baseline. This approach can detect new attacks but may generate false positives by misclassifying legitimate activity as malicious. Modern anomaly-based IDS uses machine learning, deep learning, and artificial neural networks to improve performance.
- **Hybrid IDS**: Combine signature and anomaly-based detection approaches.

3.1.4 IDS Placement Strategies

- **Centralized IDS:** Analysis and intrusion detection are carried out by a single manager.
- **Distributed IDS:** Monitoring modules are deployed across the network.

3.1.5 AI and Machine Learning in IDS

The integration of AI and machine learning significantly enhances the capabilities of IDS. Machine learning algorithms can analyze large volumes of data to identify patterns and anomalies indicative of potential security breaches. AI-driven IDS improves adaptability, allowing systems to evolve and respond to new threats in real-time without manual intervention. Behavioral analysis-based IDS are gaining traction as a reliable means to detect network anomalies. These systems understand the baseline behavior of an organization's network or device by analyzing data from multiple sources, such as network traffic logs, system logs, and user activity logs.

3.1.6 Challenges and Research Directions

Despite the advancements in IDS forIoT, several challenges remain.

- **Security Issues**: IoT devices increase and security issues are posed in all three layers of the IoT architecture.
- **Resource Constraints**: IoT devices often have limited processing power and memory, making it challenging to implement complex IDS.
- **Diversity of Devices**: The heterogeneity of IoT devices and protocols complicates the design of universal IDS solutions.
- **Data Volume**: The massive amount of data generated by IoT devices requires scalable IDS architectures.

Ongoing research focuses on developing lightweight IDS algorithms, utilizing edge computing to distribute processing, and incorporating AI to improve detection accuracy and reduce false positives.

Video Resources
https://www.youtube.com/watch?v=Oii2OsWt1sg

Use of ICT

The use of Information and Communication Technology (ICT) in IoT Intrusion Detection Systems (IDS) is essential for enhancing security in interconnected environments. ICT enables the collection and analysis of vast amounts of IoT network data, facilitating the deployment of advanced IDS models such as anomaly-based, signature-based, and hybrid approaches to detect threats like Denial-of-Service (DoS) attacks. With edge computing integration, ICT supports real-time intrusion detection by processing data closer to IoT devices, reducing latency and improving responsiveness. Additionally, ICT infrastructure provides computational resources for implementing optimization techniques like Particle Swarm Optimization (PSO) and Bat algorithms, which enhance feature selection and model accuracy. By leveraging ICT tools, IoT IDS can adapt to resource-constrained environments while ensuring robust security across application, network, and physical layers in IoT systems.

3.2 CLOUD-BASED IDS: CHALLENGES AND SOLUTIONS

Cloud computing's open and distributed nature makes it vulnerable to attacks, making security a major concern for organizations. Cloud-based Intrusion Detection Systems (CIDS) as given in figure 3.2 are designed to protect cloud environments from these threats, but they also come with their own set of challenges.

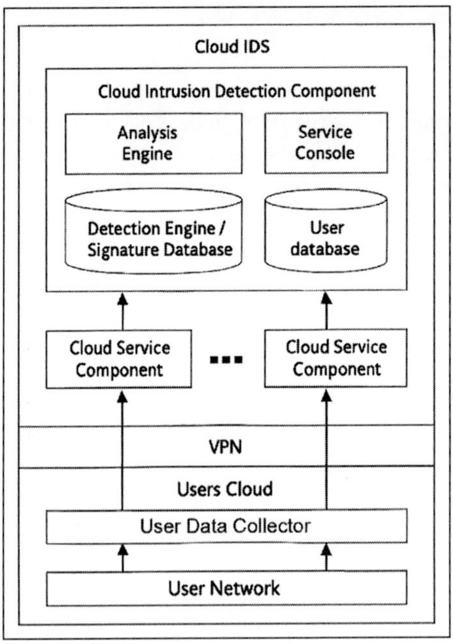

Figure 3.2.: *Cloud Based Intrusion Detection System Framework*

CBIDS framework consists of three principal components; namely, User Data Collector (UDC), Cloud Service Component (CSC), and Cloud Intrusion Detection Component (CIDC). Communication among UDC and CSC which contains confidential information for forwarding purposes is encrypted.

User Data Collector (UDC)

The UDC is a secured independent server which contains collection of necessary information. UDC is integrated inside the user Clouds based on user requirements to protect the whole network efficiently. UDC is responsible to standardize and filtered the collection of packets information before being forwarded to Cloud IDS through a secure VPN connection.

Cloud Service Component (CSC)

CSC is in charge of analyzing and validating the received information from UDC to figure out external intrusion before determining whether to delete these information or forward them to appropriate analysis engine inside the Cloud Intrusion Detection Component (CIDC). CSC is also responsible for translating the received information into a common format which is understood by the CIDC.

Cloud Intrusion Detection Component (CIDC)

CIDC is considered as the principal component for intrusion detection. There are four important modules in CIDC; namely, the Analysis Engine, Service Console, Signature Database and User Database.

Analysis Engine (AE)

AE works as a pattern matching mechanism. It is responsible for data analysis process which came from CSC and matches the data with patterns stored in the signature database. AE is an independent process which can be any IDS, e.g. Snort. AE identifies intrusion activities and generates alerts through the service console.

Service Console (SC)

SC is the remote user preferred service controller. CIDC can be configured for fine tuning based on user demands through SC. SC also handle the user authentication which has privileged access to CIDC.

Malicious activities will be reported to the user through SC. Usually, IDS alerts are in different formats, and SC represents all the alerts in a common format called Intrusion Detection Message Exchange Format (IDMEF).

Signature Database (SDB)

SDB contains the entire up-to-date attack signatures.

User Database (UDB)

UDB contains user information such as login information, user activities, etc.

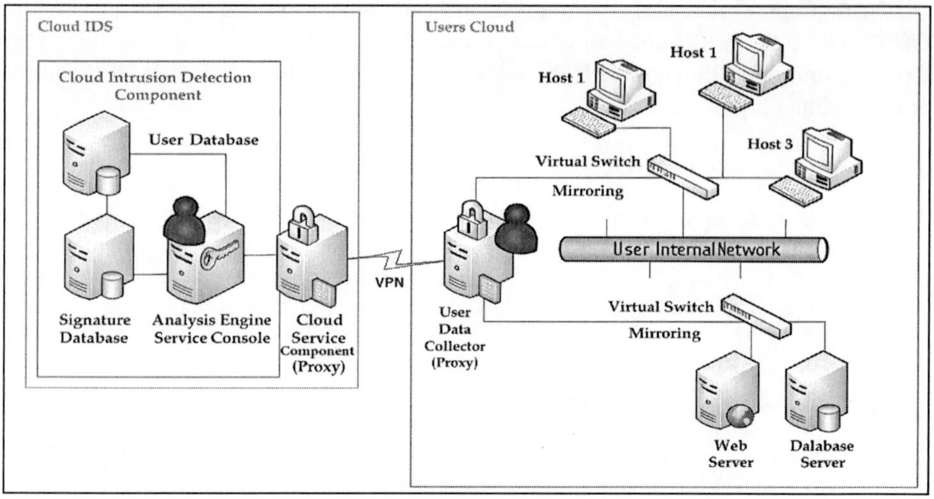

Figure 3.3.: *CBIDS Sample Architecture*

Figure 3.3. represents the sample scenario architecture based on CBIDS framework. We target Small and Medium Enterprises (SMEs) as the client (Users). The user should fulfill some requirements in order to use CBIDS. An intermediate server (proxy), VPN, virtual switch connection should be allocated on the user network. The illustrated figure comprises into two parts namely Users Cloud and Cloud IDS. The Users Cloud itself contains virtual switches, hosts, and servers which are connected through a virtual network. Several servers and hosts can be created inside the Users Cloud.

Here, we assume each single machine as a HostVM. Each Host-VM is connected to virtual switches which support SPAN features. Sensitive information for inbound and outbound traffic of each Host-VM is copied and forwarded to the UDC (proxy). Later, the UDC gathers this information and forwards it to the Cloud CSC (proxy) which resides in the IDS Cloud through a secure VPN connection. The IDS Cloud provides a comprehensive global defensive mechanism and detects the entire attacks based on the information forwarded by the user in real time. The types of Cloud Based IDS is as given in figure 3.4

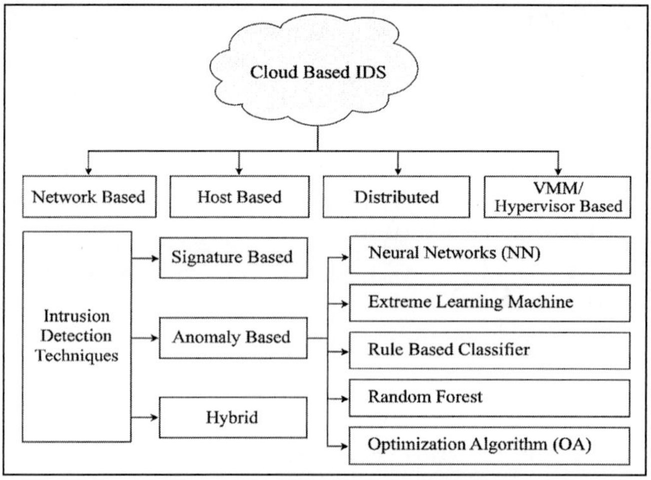

Figure 3.4.: *Types of Cloud Based IDS*

When the packets arrive at the CSC, the CSC will proceed to verify and filter the entire information before forwarding the necessary and appropriate information to the AE. The AE matches the appropriate information with the attack signatures stored in the signature database (SDB). After the analyzing process, the AE will produce a report or event to the UC for the user's attention and further action. Users are also provided with specific access into the Cloud IDS through a web-enabled service (UC) to configure and update their service requirements.

3.2.1 Challenges of Cloud-based IDS

- **Security Vulnerabilities**: The cloud environment's open and distributed nature makes it prone to security threats and vulnerabilities.
- **Data Control:** Users accessing data on remote servers without responsibility for data storage and maintenance raises concerns about data integrity, confidentiality, and availability.
- **Adaptability**: Some CIDS struggle to adapt to high access rates in the cloud network.
- **Detection of New Attacks:** Many CIDS are vulnerable to detecting new and distributed attacks.
- **Lack of Control**: Users may experience a lack of control over the CIDS.
- **High Volume of Alerts**: Intrusion detection solutions can generate a large number of alerts, which can be a burden for internal teams. Many of these alerts are false positives, & organizations may lack the time and resources to investigate each one.
- **Effective Deployment**: Ensuring the correct installation and optimization of intrusion detection solutions can be tricky, and if not done well, critical assets may be exposed.

3.2.2 Solutions for Cloud-based IDS

- **Integrated CIDS**: An integrated CIDS can monitor the entire cloud network, detect intrusions, and log events.
- **Ensemble Systems**: Utilizing an enhanced bagging ensemble system of deep learning models can effectively predict intrusions.
- **Third-Party Cloud Service**: Introducing a third-party cloud service can provide transparency and control to cloud users. A third-party Cloud-based Intrusion Detection System Service (CIDSS) can also monitor the proposed CIDS and provide reporting services.
- **Feature Extraction**: Implementing an auditing system that captures data flow and extracts features for training and building prediction models.
- **Machine Learning**: Cloud-based intrusion detection models can use machine learning techniques like random forest (RF) and feature engineering to enhance accuracy.
- **Baselining Behaviors**: Additional work is needed to baseline behaviors specific to each environment.
- **Cloud-based intrusion detection system (IDS)**: Essential for companies migrating workloads and services to public cloud infrastructure like Amazon Web Services (AWS) and Microsoft® Azure.

Video Resources
https://www.youtube.com/watch?v=jqP9isLvRLo

Use of ICT

The use of Information and Communication Technology (ICT) in cloud-based Intrusion Detection Systems (IDS) addresses the unique challenges posed by dynamic and distributed cloud environments. ICT enables real-time monitoring and analysis of network traffic across cloud infrastructures, leveraging scalable and elastic architectures to detect threats like malware, spyware, and command-and-control attacks. Cloud-native IDS solutions utilize ICT tools such as virtual network taps, APIs, and automated threat intelligence updates to provide comprehensive visibility into intra- and inter-VPC communications. ICT supports painless deployment models, including Software as a Service (SaaS) offerings and Secure Access Service Edge (SASE) solutions, ensuring seamless integration with existing security frameworks. Additionally, advanced ICT infrastructures facilitate continuous threat intelligence updates and high-performance detection mechanisms powered by machine learning and signature-based approaches to address evolving cyber threats. By leveraging ICT, cloud-based IDS solutions offer scalable, efficient, and proactive security for modern cloud environments while minimizing management overhead.

3.3 INTRUSION DETECTION IN BLOCKCHAIN NETWORKS

Blockchain technology's decentralized nature introduces unique security challenges, making traditional security measures inadequate for detecting and preventing intrusions. The absence of a dedicated Intrusion Detection System (IDS) designed for blockchain networks leaves these systems susceptible to attacks. However, blockchain itself can enhance the security and integrity of intrusion detection systems through its decentralized and immutable ledger.

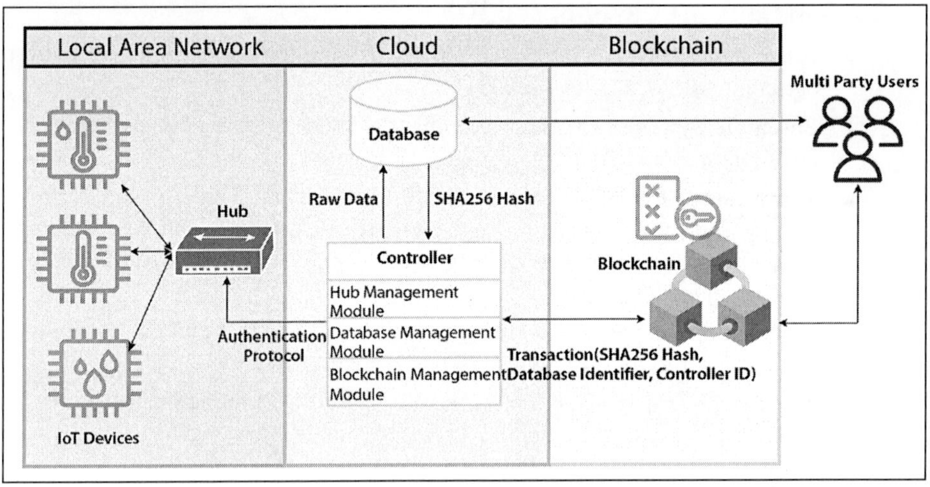

Figure 3.5.: *BlockchainSystem Overview*

In this section, we provide a brief overview of our system. The proposed system figure 5 consists of seven entities: sensors, hubs, controller, cloud, database, blockchain and users.

- **Users:** A user is one who can access IoT sensors, data analysis and validation services.

- **IoT Device:** An IoT device is a resource-constrained device that cannot run heavy cryptographic algorithms such as digital signature schemes. It is not tamper-proof, and it is connected to a device hub for networking. We assume that the connection between an IoT device and a hub is secure.
- **Hubs:** A hub gathers information from a group of IoT devices and sends authenticated messages to a cloud. It is a lightweight device, but it can perform cryptographic algorithms like hash functions.
- **Controller**: A controller collects and checks the validity of data received from hubs. It stores the validated data in an external database and updates policies (e.g., timing information) shared with the hubs. A controller can write a transaction to the blockchain periodically.
- **Cloud**: A cloud can have multiple controllers and a database that stores authenticated data collected from the hubs.
- **Database:** A database is public storage for the sensing information where a user can access their business data.
- **Blockchain:** A blockchain is used for auditing purposes, as a user can check the data (stored on the database) integrity by checking the transactions on the blockchain.

In this system, the sensors are lightweight devices without sufficient capability for cryptographic computations. These sensors are connected to the hub and continuously sense data. These data are sent to the hub where the hub collects batches of data and sends the data to the controller periodically. A hub has limited processing and storage capability, but it is relatively stronger than IoT devices.

The controller is the main entity of the system that performs multiple functions and interacts with the hubs, database and blockchain. The controller has four main modules as discussed below.

- **Device management module**: The controller provides a timing policy to the connected hubs. The novelty of the proposed system is the timing policy which is used to identify the IoT devices. The timing policy provides the individualized data transmission schedule to all the connected hubs, which is used to identify the data sent by the valid/correct hub. The timing policy also consists of the margin of noise that every hub can add during the scheduling process.

  A controller can check the validity of the received data from the hubs. The controller uses the timing information from a group of data records coming from each hub. The controller uses the timing policy to identify the hub. Noise is a random value within a margin (decided by the controller) that is added to the scheduling interval by the hub. The controller uses an error correction technique to remove the noise correctly and identify the hub.
- **Database management module:** After identifying the source hub the SHA256 hash of the data is calculated, and the data is stored in the database. When the data is stored in the database, the index of the data is sent back to the controller.
- **Blockchain management module**: Controllers are blockchain nodes capable of generating transactions. The transaction includes SHA256 hash of the data, controller ID and the database identifier that includes database address and data index.

- **Access control module**: This module is responsible for token authentication to provide access to users.

3.3.1 How Blockchain Improves Intrusion Detection

- **Immutable Audit Trail**: Blockchain provides an unalterable and transparent audit trail, which is valuable for incident response, forensic investigations, and attribution of cyberattacks.
- **Distributed Consensus**: Blockchain fosters trust, transparency, and collaboration among stakeholders, enabling faster threat detection and response.
- **Enhanced Security and Reliability**: Blockchain's decentralized and immutable nature can enhance the security and reliability of intrusion detection systems by providing transparent and tamper-proof logs of network activity.
- **Data Privacy and Security**: Blockchain can increase data privacy and find both current and future threats in combination with intrusion detection1. A machine blockchain framework (MBF) can provide distributed intrusion detection with security and blockchain with privacy with the help of smart contracts in IoT networks.

3.3.2 Approaches to Integrating Blockchain with IDS

- **Machine Blockchain Framework (MBF)**: A system for detecting intrusions that keeps data secure and private in cloud networks.
- **Trust Management**: Fusing trust management with blockchain technology enables communication in networks without any trusted party to maintain the integrity of shared data and assists in assessing each node's trustworthiness.
- **Decentralized Environment**: A CIDS (Cloud Intrusion Detection System) with a decentralized environment emphasizes the value of developing trust among CIDS nodes.
- **Collaborative Blockchain-Based Intrusion Detection**: A framework known as BlockCSDN can be used for collaborative blockchain-based intrusion detection in SDN, using the CIDS of challenge-based as a case study.

3.3.3 Challenges and Future Directions

- **Novel Security Challenges:** The proliferation of blockchain technology has introduced novel security challenges, necessitating the development of specialized solutions.
- **Unique Attack Surface:** The inherent characteristics of blockchain, such as transparency and decentralization, create a unique attack surface that demands a tailored approach to intrusion detection.
- **Evolving Technology**: As blockchain technology continues to evolve, further research and development in integrating blockchain with intrusion detection will unlock new possibilities for combating cyber threats.
- **Insider Threats**: Blockchain technology has the capability to improve the trust management enhancing the detection of malware in the insider nodes.
- **Alarm Aggregation**: Blockchain improves alarm aggregation aspects of challenge-based CIDNs (i.e., identifying untruthful inputs).

Video Resources
https://www.youtube.com/watch?v=fUMWwDYPjOk

Use of ICT

The use of Information and Communication Technology (ICT) for intrusion detection in blockchain networks enhances security, transparency, and resilience against cyber threats. Blockchain technology, supported by ICT, provides decentralized and immutable data storage, ensuring tamper-proof logs of network activity for effective forensic investigations and incident response. ICT facilitates the integration of blockchain with advanced intrusion detection systems (IDS), enabling collaborative detection networks where nodes exchange data securely to identify malicious activities in real-time. Robust cryptographic mechanisms within blockchain, powered by ICT tools, protect data integrity and foster trust among stakeholders, improving threat detection and response times. Furthermore, ICT supports scalable blockchain-based IDS frameworks that leverage AI and machine learning algorithms to analyze complex attack patterns and enhance detection accuracy in resource-constrained environments like IoT and industrial networks. By combining blockchain's transparency with ICT's computational capabilities, modern IDS can address challenges such as evolving threats and trust management while ensuring sustainable cybersecurity solutions for smart cities and industrial systems.

3.4 MOBILE AND WIRELESS NETWORK IDS

Wireless intrusion detection systems (WIDS) and wireless intrusion protection systems (WIPS) are used to continuously protect a wireless network, and in some cases, a wired network, from unauthorized users. A WIDS uses a system of sensors to monitor the network for the intrusion of unauthorized devices, such as rogue access points. A WIPS not only detects unauthorized devices but also takes steps to mitigate the threat by containing the device and detaching it from the wireless network. The IDS architecture of Wireless Mobile Networks is as shown in figure 3.6.

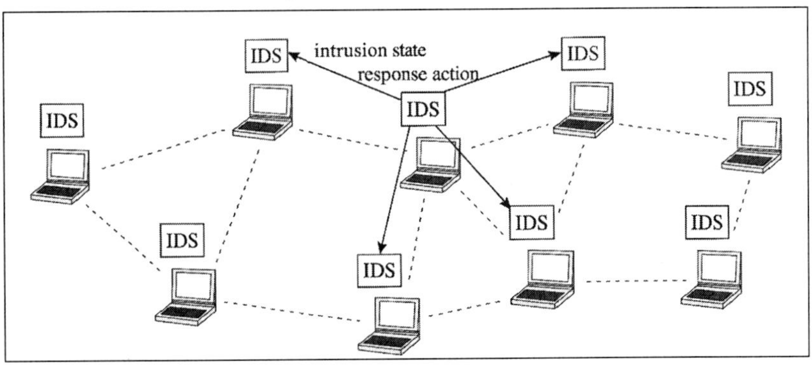

***Figure 3.6.:** IDS Architecture of Wireless Mobile Networks*

3.4.1 Key Aspects of WIDS and WIPS

- **Continuous Protection**: WIDS and WIPS operate 24/7 and guard the wireless local area network (WLAN) on a constant basis, listening to all radio traffic within the WLAN's operating frequencies.

- **Components:** A typical WIPS has three components: a server, a management console, and a collection of distributed sensors. The WIPS server performs system management and configuration tasks, signature, behavior, and protocol analysis, as well as radio frequency (RF) spectrum analysis to detect intrusion.
- **Functionality**: Most available systems fundamentally act as a WIPS because they are designed to detect and prevent wireless intrusion.
- **Detection Mechanisms**: The integration of both signature-based and anomaly-based detection mechanisms enhances the overall effectiveness of intrusion detection, allowing the system to detect known attack patterns as well as abnormal behaviors that may indicate novel threats.
- **Adaptability**: Designed to be adaptable to evolving threats, the combination of signature-based and anomaly-based detection mechanisms ensures flexibility in identifying both known and unknown intrusion attempts, making it resilient to emerging attack vectors.

3.4.2 Types of Analysis Used

Signature analysis monitors traffic for patterns associated with known attacks, such as denial of service (DoS) and man-in-the-middle attacks. Behavior analysis looks for anomalies in message behavior such as the use of purposefully malformed management frames that allow an attacker to observe the network's resulting behavior, and compares historical usage metrics to anomalous traffic to indicate unusual traffic that may be an attempt to probe vulnerable systems.Protocol analysis is used to inspect and disassemble layer-2 information to discover anomalies in the frame header and trailer, and dissects the layer 3 to 7 data contained in the frame body for spurious data that could be leveraged to compromise the security or medium arbitration functions of the system.RF Spectrum analysis is used to monitor the frequency on which the system is operating for unwanted or damaging signals and identify and locate sources of interference, whether malicious or otherwise.

3.4.3 WLAN Devices

Authorized devices are those devices that have been authenticated as valid clients through the access security methods being used and are authorized to access WLAN resources. Unauthorized devices are those devices that are not rogues but have been detected and are not authenticated to the protected WLAN.Neighbor device is a known device that is associated with a neighboring AP belonging to a nearby business or other entity.Rogue device is an unauthorized device that is either deliberately interfering with the operation of the WLAN or is considered a viable threat to the network. After an unauthorized device is found to be a rogue device, it is formally classified as such, and the WIPS typically uses spoofed de-authentication frames to terminate the rogue device's ability to connect to any other device.

Video Resources
https://www.youtube.com/watch?v=F4t7PpKZV3U

Use of ICT

The use of Information and Communication Technology (ICT) for mobile and wireless network Intrusion Detection Systems (IDS) enhances security by enabling real-time monitoring, analysis, and response to cyber threats in dynamic and resource-constrained environments. ICT facilitates the deployment of advanced IDS frameworks that leverage machine learning and hybrid detection techniques to identify both known and unknown attacks, such as Distributed Denial of Service (DDoS) and blackhole attacks, in mobile ad hoc networks (MANETs) and wireless sensor networks (WSNs). Edge computing, a key ICT component, reduces latency by processing intrusion detection tasks closer to the data source, improving responsiveness and scalability in mobile environments. ICT also supports the integration of open-source tools like Kismet for wireless traffic analysis, enabling cost-effective and vendor-independent solutions for detecting unauthorized access points and malicious activities. Additionally, ICT-driven IDS frameworks incorporate secure communication layers and cryptographic measures to protect against attacks targeting the IDS itself, ensuring robustness in mobile and wireless networks.

3.5 TRENDS IN LIGHTWEIGHT IDS FOR RESOURCE-CONSTRAINED ENVIRONMENTS

As the Internet of Things (IoT) continues to proliferate, the need for effective security solutions tailored to resource-constrained environments has become increasingly critical. Lightweight Intrusion Detection Systems (IDS) are designed to operate efficiently on devices with limited computational power, memory, and battery life. This section explores the current trends in lightweight IDS, highlighting their significance and the methodologies employed to enhance their effectiveness.

1. Machine Learning Techniques

Machine learning (ML) has emerged as a key component in developing lightweight IDS. By leveraging ML algorithms, researchers can create systems that not only detect intrusions but also adapt to evolving threats. Recent studies have demonstrated the effectiveness of various ML techniques in enhancing the performance of lightweight IDS.

- **Feature Selection**: Lightweight IDS often employ feature selection methods to reduce computational overhead. Filter-based methods are particularly favored due to their low computational cost. By selecting only the most relevant features, these systems can operate more efficiently without sacrificing detection accuracy.
- **Classification Algorithms**: Various classification algorithms have been tested for lightweight IDS, including Decision Trees (DT), k-Nearest Neighbors (KNN), and Support Vector Machines (SVM). Among these, Decision Trees have shown promising results due to their balance between performance and resource consumption.

2. Behavioral Analysis

Behavioral analysis-based intrusion detection is gaining traction as a reliable method for detecting anomalies in network traffic. These systems establish a baseline of normal behavior by analyzing historical data and then monitor for deviations that may indicate an intrusion.

- **Anomaly Detection**: Lightweight IDS increasingly incorporate anomaly detection techniques that utilize behavioral patterns to identify potential threats. This approach allows for the detection of previously unknown attacks (zero-day exploits) that traditional signature-based systems may miss.

- **Data Fusion**: Combining data from multiple sources—such as network traffic logs, system logs, and user activity—enhances the accuracy of behavioral analysis. This fusion of data helps create a more comprehensive view of network activity and improves the likelihood of detecting malicious behavior.

3. Edge Computing Integration

The integration of edge computing with lightweight IDS is a significant trend aimed at addressing latency and bandwidth issues inherent in cloud-based solutions.

- **Local Processing**: By processing data closer to where it is generated (at the edge), lightweight IDS can reduce latency and improve response times. This is particularly important for IoT devices that require immediate action to mitigate threats.
- **Resource Optimization**: Edge computing allows for better resource allocation, enabling lightweight IDS to function effectively within constrained environments without overwhelming the device's capabilities.

4. UltrA. Lightweight Approaches

Recent research has focused on developing ultra-lightweight intrusion detection systems specifically designed for massive IoT networks.

- **Deep-Packet Analysis**: Some approaches utilize deep-packet analysis techniques that model payloads using n-gram bit-patterns, allowing for efficient detection of anomalies while minimizing resource consumption1. This method is particularly effective for small IoT devices with limited processing power.
- **Distributed Architectures**: Implementing distributed architectures where multiple lightweight IDS collaborate can enhance detection capabilities while sharing the processing load across devices. This approach helps maintain performance without compromising security.

5. Automation and Real-Time Response

Automation plays a crucial role in enhancing the efficiency of lightweight IDS.

- **Automated Threat Response**: Lightweight IDS are increasingly incorporating automated response mechanisms that allow them to take predefined actions when an intrusion is detected, such as isolating affected devices or alerting administrators. This rapid response capability is essential for mitigating damage from attacks.
- **Continuous Learning**: Machine learning algorithms enable continuous learning from new data, allowing lightweight IDS to adapt over time and improve their detection capabilities without requiring extensive manual intervention.

The evolution of lightweight intrusion detection systems is critical in addressing the unique challenges posed by resource-constrained environments, particularly within IoT networks. By leveraging machine learning techniques, behavioral analysis, edge computing integration, ultra-lightweight approaches, and automation, these systems are becoming increasingly effective at detecting and responding to intrusions while operating within limited resources. As cyber threats continue to evolve, ongoing research and development in this field will be essential for maintaining robust security in an increasingly connected world.

Video Resources
https://www.youtube.com/watch?v=RuhNpsRZHcU

Use of ICT

The use of Information and Communication Technology (ICT) for lightweight Intrusion Detection Systems (IDS) in resource-constrained environments is critical for ensuring security while maintaining efficiency. ICT enables the deployment of optimized IDS models, such as DNN-BiLSTM with dynamic quantization, which reduce computational complexity and memory usage without compromising detection accuracy, making them suitable for IoT devices with limited resources1. Advanced ICT tools support feature dimensionality reduction techniques like Incremental Principal Component Analysis (IPCA), which streamline data preprocessing and allow real-time monitoring in IoT networks. ICT also facilitates the integration of lightweight IDS with Multi-Access Edge Computing (MEC) to process data closer to the source, reducing latency and enhancing responsiveness in detecting threats. Additionally, ICT aids in the implementation of hyperparameter optimization frameworks like Optuna, which improve model performance while keeping energy consumption low, ensuring scalability and adaptability in diverse IoT ecosystems. By leveraging ICT, lightweight IDS can balance resource constraints with robust threat detection, ensuring secure operations in environments like smart homes, industrial IoT, and healthcare systems.

3.6 CASE STUDY: SECURING EMERGING TECHNOLOGIES AT GLOBAL TECH INNOVATIONS

1. Securing IoT Devices with Blockchain Technology (Samsung)

- **Challenge**: Samsung faced difficulties in protecting its IoT devices from escalating cyber threats due to the decentralized and diverse nature of IoT networks.
- **Solution:** They used blockchain to secure IoT devices, creating a decentralized ledger for each device to record transactions and data exchanges securely, preventing unauthorized tampering.
- **Impact**: This ensured the integrity of device communications and data exchanges, decreasing the risk of tampering and increased consumer trust.

2. Revolutionizing Threat Detection with AI-Powered Security Systems (Palo Alto Networks)

- **Challenge**: Palo Alto Networks struggled to manage security data and keep pace with evolving cyber threats, as traditional methods faltered against advanced malware.
- **Solution**: They introduced an AI-powered security platform that uses machine learning algorithms to analyze network data, automating threat detection.
- **Impact**: This improved threat detection rates and decreased the time from detection to resolution. It also allowed them to offer more robust security solutions to a larger client base.

3. Innovation in Cybersecurity for Critical National Infrastructure

- **Challenge**: Critical National Infrastructure (CNI) faces severe cyber threats due to increasing internet exposure. This includes difficulty distinguishing legitimate from fraudulent transactions and weaknesses in traditional firewalls.
- **Solution:** A multi-layered cybersecurity strategy was implemented, including blockchain for data integrity, AI-powered threat detectors, a Zero Trust Architecture, and quantum cryptographic algorithms.
- **Impact**: This resulted in enhanced data integrity, proactive threat detection, improved security access management, and future-proofing against quantum threats.

4. Enhancing Cloud Security with Automated Compliance Tools (Amazon Web Services)

- **Challenge**: AWS needed to ensure compliance with international security standards to protect customer data.
- **Solution:** They introduced automated compliance tools into its cloud platform, which continuously monitor and audit AWS services against global standards.
- **Impact:** This streamlined compliance processes, reduced manual workload, and helped maintain high-security standards.

Video Resources
https://www.youtube.com/watch?v=9AJHTW4o5z0

Use of ICT

The use of Information and Communication Technology (ICT) in securing emerging technologies at Global Tech Innovations is pivotal for addressing the evolving landscape of cybersecurity threats. ICT enables the integration of advanced tools such as blockchain technology for ensuring data integrity and preventing tampering, while AI and machine learning algorithms automate threat detection and identify attack patterns in real-time. Zero Trust architectures, supported by ICT, enforce strict access controls and identity verification to minimize both external and internal threats.

Additionally, ICT facilitates the deployment of quantum cryptographic algorithms to future-proof systems against quantum computing threats, ensuring long-term security for sensitive digital infrastructures. By leveraging ICT, organizations can enhance operational efficiency, proactively detect threats, and secure critical assets across sectors like energy, healthcare, and telecommunications.

SUMMARY

- **IoT Intrusion Detection Systems**: Focus on addressing security challenges in IoT environments by implementing lightweight and efficient IDS solutions to overcome resource constraints and dynamic threats.
- **Cloud-Based IDS: Challenges and Solutions**: Analyze scalability, latency, and data privacy issues in cloud-based IDS while exploring innovative solutions like distributed detection mechanisms.

- **Intrusion Detection in Blockchain Networks**: Highlight the integration of IDS with blockchain technology to secure decentralized networks and enhance transparency in peer-to-peer transactions.
- **Mobile and Wireless Network IDS**: Discuss IDS approaches tailored for mobile and wireless networks, emphasizing lightweight models to handle limited computational resources and dynamic attack scenarios.
- **Case Study: Securing Emerging Technologies at GlobalTech Innovations**: Showcase real-world applications of AI-driven IDS in protecting modern technologies like IoT, cloud, and blockchain networks against sophisticated cyber threats.

EXERCISES

A. Subjective Questions

Category-I (Revised Bloom's Levels-1, 2 & 3)

1. Define IoT Intrusion Detection Systems and explain their importance in securing resource-constrained environments.
2. Describe the challenges faced by cloud-based IDS and discuss potential solutions for overcoming scalability and latency issues.
3. Explain the role of blockchain technology in enhancing IDS performance in decentralized networks.
4. List key features of lightweight IDS solutions for mobile and wireless networks.
5. Summarize the case study on "Securing Emerging Technologies at GlobalTech Innovations" and its impact on modern cybersecurity strategies.

Category-II (Revised Bloom's Levels-4, 5 & 6)

1. Analyze how blockchain-based IDS can mitigate security threats in IoT networks while addressing resource constraints.
2. Design a framework for implementing lightweight IDS in mobile and wireless networks, considering computational limitations.
3. Evaluate the effectiveness of cloud-based IDS solutions in large-scale enterprise environments using real-world examples.
4. Propose improvements to blockchain-integrated IDS for securing IoT devices against sophisticated cyberattacks like DDoS.
5. Critically assess the trends in lightweight IDS solutions for emerging technologies and suggest future directions for research.

B. Objective Questions

Category-I (Revised Bloom's Levels-1, 2 & 3)

1. What is a major challenge for IoT Intrusion Detection Systems?
   (a) High computational power requirements
   (b) Resource constraints in IoT devices
   (c) Lack of network scalability
   (d) Inefficient data storage

2. Which technology is used to ensure sensing data integrity in IoT networks?
   (a) Artificial Intelligence
   (b) Blockchain technology
   (c) Cloud computing
   (d) Machine learning
3. What is the primary function of smart contracts in blockchain-based IDS?
   (a) Encrypting data packets
   (b) Automating predefined rules and conditions
   (c) Managing network traffic flow
   (d) Validating device configurations
4. Lightweight IDS are primarily designed for which type of environments?
   (a) High-performance cloud systems
   (b) Resource-constrained networks
   (c) Large-scale enterprise networks
   (d) Decentralized blockchain systems
5. What security threat does blockchain-based IDS help mitigate in IoT networks?
   (a) SQL injection attacks
   (b) Distributed Denial of Service (DDoS) attacks
   (c) Malware propagation
   (d) Phishing attacks

Ans.: 1. (b), 2. (b), 3. (b), 4. (b), 5. (b)

Category-II *(Revised Bloom's Levels-4, 5 & 6)*

1. Which consensus algorithm is most suitable for lightweight blockchain-based IDS in IoT environments?
   (a) Proof of Work (PoW)
   (b) Delegated Proof of Stake (DPoS)
   (c) Byzantine Fault Tolerance (BFT)
   (d) Crash Fault Tolerance (CFT)
2. What is a key advantage of integrating blockchain with cloud-based IDS?
   (a) Reduced latency in data transmission
   (b) Enhanced transparency and immutability
   (c) Improved computational efficiency
   (d) Simplified network architecture
3. Identify the most effective method to secure mobile networks using lightweight IDS:
   (a) Implementing signature-based detection algorithms
   (b) Using AI-driven anomaly detection techniques
   (c) Deploying centralized monitoring systems
   (d) Encrypting all network traffic
4. Which emerging trend enhances lightweight IDS performance in resource-constrained environments?
   (a) Integration with AI-driven analytics tools
   (b) Use of permissionlessblockchain networks
   (c) Deployment on high-power cloud platforms
   (d) Adoption of traditional rule-based systems

5. How does GlobalTech Innovations secure emerging technologies using AI-enabled IDS? *(Open-ended MCQ with justification)*

Ans.: 1. (b), 2. (b), 3. (b), 4. (a)

TEACHER'S KNOW MORE

To effectively teach the topics in this chapter, educators should focus on the unique challenges and advancements in Intrusion Detection Systems (IDS) for emerging technologies. IoT-based IDS must address resource constraints, heterogeneous devices, and dynamic threats, often leveraging lightweight machine learning or deep learning models to optimize performance. Cloud-based IDS face scalability and latency issues but benefit from distributed detection mechanisms and advanced privacy-preserving techniques. Blockchain-integrated IDS enhance security through decentralized and immutable architectures, while mobile and wireless network IDS require lightweight solutions to handle limited computational resources and dynamic attack surfaces. Educators can also highlight trends in lightweight IDS for resource-constrained environments, emphasizing innovative approaches like edge computing and AI-driven anomaly detection. The case study on "Securing Emerging Technologies at GlobalTech Innovations" provides a practical perspective on implementing AI-enabled IDS to protect IoT, cloud, and blockchain networks from sophisticated cyber threats, offering a comprehensive understanding of real-world applications.

Intentionally Left Blank!

Advanced Techniques and Hybrid Models

4

UNIT

RATIONALE

This chapter focuses on advanced techniques and hybrid models in Intrusion Detection Systems (IDS) to address modern cybersecurity challenges. It begins with the application of fuzzy logic and genetic algorithms to enhance detection accuracy and adaptability. Hybrid IDS models are explored, combining signature-based and anomaly-based methods to leverage the strengths of both approaches for detecting known and unknown threats. Distributed IDS for large-scale networks is discussed, emphasizing scalability and real-time monitoring in complex environments. The chapter also covers intrusion response and alert correlation systems to improve decision-making and reduce false positives. Real-time IDS with big data analytics is introduced, showcasing how advanced analytics can process vast amounts of data for timely threat detection. A case study on "SecureNet Technologies" illustrates the implementation of these advanced techniques in a financial institution, providing practical insights into securing critical infrastructures against sophisticated cyber threats.

OUTCOMES

- **Understand Fuzzy Logic and Genetic Algorithms in IDS**: Enhance detection accuracy.
- **Analyze Hybrid IDS Models**: Combine signature-based and anomaly-based methods.
- **Design Distributed IDS for Large-Scale Networks**: Ensure scalability and efficiency.
- **Evaluate Intrusion Response and Alert Correlation Systems**: Improve decision-making.
- **Apply Real-Time IDS with Big Data Analytics**: Enable timely threat detection.

4.1 FUZZY LOGIC AND GENETIC ALGORITHMS IN IDS

Fuzzy logic and genetic algorithms as given in figure 4.1 play a significant role in enhancing the effectiveness of Intrusion Detection Systems (IDS) by addressing the challenges posed by evolving cyber threats. Fuzzy logic provides a robust mechanism for handling uncertainty and imprecision in intrusion detection by defining fuzzy rules, such as "if-then" statements, to classify network behavior as normal or anomalous. This approach is particularly useful in environments where clear boundaries between normal and malicious activities are difficult to establish. Genetic algorithms complement fuzzy logic by optimizing fuzzy membership functions, feature selection, and rule generation, ensuring that the IDS adapts dynamically to new attack patterns. Together, these techniques create hybrid systems capable of detecting both known and unknown intrusions with high accuracy while reducing false alarm rates. The integration of fuzzy logic and genetic algorithms into IDS has been tested on benchmark datasets like KDD'99, demonstrating significant improvements in precision and efficiency. For example, fuzzy data mining techniques extract patterns of normal behavior from network audit data, while genetic algorithms refine these patterns to enhance detection capabilities. This combination also supports anomaly-based intrusion detection by identifying deviations from established norms and misuse detection by recognizing predefined attack signatures.

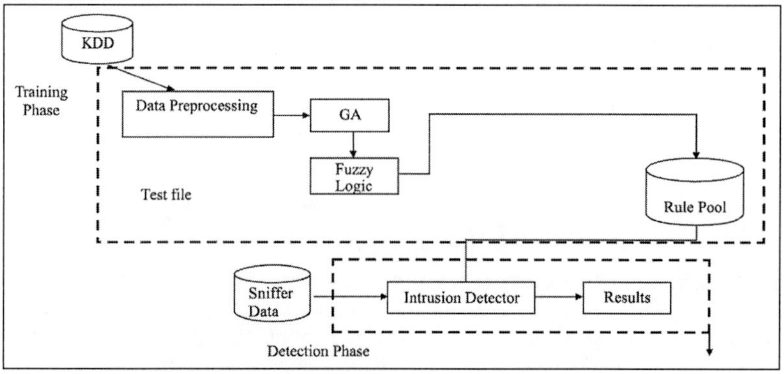

Figure 4.1: *Fuzzy Genetic Algorithm*

Furthermore, these methods are computationally efficient, making them suitable for real-time applications in complex network environments. By leveraging the strengths of both fuzzy logic and genetic algorithms, modern IDS can provide adaptable and scalable security solutions for protecting critical systems against sophisticated cyber threats.

4.1.1 Mathematical Explanation of Fuzzy Logic and Genetic Algorithms in IDS

Fuzzy logic and genetic algorithms combine to enhance Intrusion Detection Systems (IDS) by leveraging fuzzy rules for anomaly detection and genetic optimization for feature selection and rule tuning.

4.1.1.1 Fuzzy Logic in IDS

Fuzzy logic uses membership functions to classify data into categories like "normal" or "anomalous." A typical fuzzy rule might look like–

IF (Packet Size is High) AND (Response Time is Slow), THEN (Anomaly Level is H)

The membership function μ(x) defines the degree to which a value belongs to a fuzzy set, such as

$$\mu(x) = \frac{1}{1+e^{-k(x-c)}} \tag{1}$$

where k controls the slope and c is the centre of the fuzzy set. These functions allow IDS to handle uncertainity and overlapping data patterns effectively.

4.1.1.2 Genetic Algorithms in IDS

Genetic algorithms optimize the selection of features and fuzzy rules by iteratively improving a population of solutions. The fitness function evaluates each solution based on its accuracy in detecting intrusions. For example:

$$Fitness = \frac{\text{True Positives} + \text{True Negatives}}{\text{Total Samples}}$$

The key operations include:

- **Selection:** Choosing the best-performing solutions.
- **Crossover:** Combining two solutions to create new ones.
- **Mutation:** Randomly altering parts of a solution to explore new possibilities.

4.1.1.3 Python Program: Fuzzy Logic and Genetic Algorithm for IDS

```
importnumpyas np
importskfuzzyas fuzz
fromskfuzzyimport control as ctrl
import random
# Define Fuzzy Variables
packet_size=ctrl.Antecedent(np.arange(0,101,1),'packet_size')
response_time=ctrl.Antecedent(np.arange(0,101,1),'response_time')
anomaly_level=ctrl.Consequent(np.arange(0,101,1),'anomaly_level')
# Membership Functions
packet_size['low']=fuzz.trimf(packet_size.universe,[0,0,50])
packet_size['high']=fuzz.trimf(packet_size.universe,[50,100,100])
response_time['slow']=fuzz.trimf(response_time.universe,[50,100,100])
response_time['fast']=fuzz.trimf(response_time.universe,[0,0,50])
anomaly_level['low']=fuzz.trimf(anomaly_level.universe,[0,0,50])
anomaly_level['high']=fuzz.trimf(anomaly_level.universe,[50,100,100])
# Fuzzy Rules
rule1     =ctrl.Rule(packet_size['high']&response_time['slow'],anomaly_
level['high'])
rule2      =ctrl.Rule(packet_size['low']|response_time['fast'],anomaly_
level['low'])
# Control System
anomaly_ctrl=ctrl.ControlSystem([rule1, rule2])
anomaly_detection=ctrl.ControlSystemSimulation(anomaly_ctrl)
# Genetic Algorithm for Optimization
deffitness_function(rules):
# Simulate detection accuracy (example fitness calculation)
returnrandom.uniform(0.8,1.0)
defgenetic_algorithm(pop_size=10, generations=5):
    population =[random.sample(range(10),5)for _ inrange(pop_size)]
for gen inrange(generations):
fitness_scores=[fitness_function(individual)for      individual       in
population]
sorted_population=[x for _, x insorted(zip(fitness_scores, population),
reverse=True)]
# Selection
        selected =sorted_population[:pop_size//2]
```

```
# Crossover
    offspring =[]
foriinrange(len(selected)//2):
    parent1, parent2 = selected[i], selected[-i-1]
crossover_point=random.randint(1,len(parent1)-1)
    child = parent1[:crossover_point]+ parent2[crossover_point:]
offspring.append(child)
# Mutation
mutated_offspring=[[gene   ifrandom.random()>0.1elserandom.randint(0,9)
for gene in child]for child in offspring]
    population = selected +mutated_offspring
returnsorted_population[0]# Return best individual
# Run Genetic Algorithm
best_solution=genetic_algorithm()
print("Optimized Rules:",best_solution)
```

4.1.1.4 Key Features of the Program

- ✓ **Fuzzy Logic:** Defines membership functions and rules to classify network behavior as normal or anomalous.
- ✓ **Genetic Algorithm:** Optimizes the fuzzy rules by simulating evolution through selection, crossover, and mutation.
- ✓ **Customizable Parameters:** The program allows you to adjust population size and number of generations for optimization.

This combination provides an adaptable framework for intrusion detection that balances precision and computational efficiency.

The output of the above program will depend on the random processes involved in the genetic algorithm. However, the program is designed to return the "best" solution found by the genetic algorithm after a specified number of generations. This solution is represented as a list of integers, which could symbolize optimized rules or features for the fuzzy logic system.

Here's a general idea of what the output might look like

Optimized Rules: [3, 8, 1, 9, 5]

This output indicates that the genetic algorithm has selected a particular combination of rules or features (represented by the numbers in the list) as the most effective for intrusion detection based on the simulated fitness function.

4.1.1.5 Explanation of the Output

- ✓ **Optimized Rules:** This part of the output indicates that the genetic algorithm has optimized a set of rules or features.
- ✓ **List of Numbers:** Each number in the list corresponds to a specific rule or feature that has been optimized. For example, in a more complex scenario, these numbers might represent different network features like packet size, response time, etc., or they might represent different fuzzy rules.

4.1.1.6 Real-World Interpretation

In a real-world scenario, these optimized rules would be used to refine the fuzzy logic system, potentially improving its ability to detect intrusions by focusing on the most relevant network features or behaviors.

4.1.1.7 Example Output with Fuzzy Logic Evaluation

If you were to use the optimized rules to evaluate a specific network scenario using fuzzy logic, you might see output like this:

Anomaly Level: 80

This would indicate that based on the optimized rules and fuzzy logic evaluation, the network activity has an anomaly level of 80, suggesting a high likelihood of an intrusion.

However, the provided program does not include this level of integration with fuzzy logic evaluation; it focuses solely on optimizing rules via a genetic algorithm.

4.1.2 How do Fuzzy Logic and Genetic Algorithms Improve the Detection of Zero-day Attacks?

Fuzzy logic and genetic algorithms significantly enhance the detection of zero-day attacks by addressing the challenges of uncertainty, adaptability, and optimization in intrusion detection systems (IDS). Fuzzy logic excels in handling imprecise and ambiguous data, enabling IDS to classify network traffic patterns that deviate from normal behavior as potential zero-day threats. This capability is crucial because zero-day attacks as given in figure 4.2 often exploit unknown vulnerabilities, making it difficult to rely on predefined signatures. By applying fuzzy rules, IDS can detect anomalies even in complex and uncertain environments, improving the system's ability to identify previously unseen attack vectors.

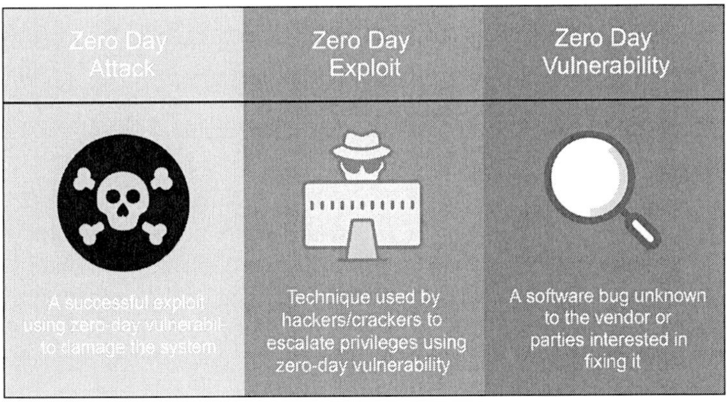

Figure 4.2.: *Zero Day Attacks*

Genetic algorithms complement fuzzy logic by optimizing the IDS's detection capabilities through evolutionary techniques. These algorithms iteratively refine fuzzy membership functions, feature selection, and rule sets to improve accuracy and reduce false positives. Genetic algorithms are particularly effective in adapting to dynamic network conditions and evolving attack strategies, ensuring that the IDS remains robust against new threats. Together, fuzzy logic and genetic algorithms create a hybrid approach that not only improves the detection of zero-day attacks but also enhances scalability and efficiency in real-time applications.

4.1.3 Role of Fuzzy Membership Functions in Anomaly Detection

Fuzzy membership functions play a crucial role in anomaly detection by quantifying the degree of membership of data points to specific classes, such as normal or anomalous behavior. These functions define the "fuzziness" or uncertainty in classifying data, enabling the system to handle ambiguous or overlapping patterns that traditional binary classification methods might miss. For example, interval-valued fuzzy membership functions, as used in audio anomaly detection, provide optimistic and pessimistic bounds for classifying events, allowing for a more nuanced evaluation of anomalies based on reconstruction errors or other metrics.

Additionally, fuzzy membership functions improve the robustness of anomaly detection systems by reducing the impact of outliers and enhancing interpretability. They can be designed using various shapes like triangular, trapezoidal, or Gaussian functions, depending on the application and data characteristics. These functions are particularly effective in dynamic or non-stationary environments where data distributions change over time, as they allow for adaptive classification and clustering of anomalies without rigid boundaries. By leveraging fuzzy membership functions, anomaly detection systems can achieve higher accuracy and flexibility in identifying rare or previously unseen patterns.

4.1.4 How can Genetic Algorithms Optimize the Feature Selection in Intrusion Detection Systems?

Genetic algorithms (GAs) optimize feature selection in intrusion detection systems (IDS) by effectively navigating the feature space to identify the most relevant attributes for classification, thereby improving detection accuracy and efficiency. GAs mimic the process of natural selection, using operations like selection, crossover, and mutation to iteratively refine a population of feature subsets. This approach ensures a balance between exploration (searching new areas of the feature space) and exploitation (refining known good solutions), enabling the IDS to avoid suboptimal solutions and adapt to diverse attack patterns. For example, in studies like the "Opt-Forest" model, GAs are employed to select optimal features that improve the compactness and accuracy of decision trees, enhancing the IDS's ability to detect sophisticated threats.

Additionally, GAs are particularly effective in high-dimensional datasets where traditional feature selection methods may struggle. They can integrate with other optimization techniques, such as Whale Optimization Algorithms (WOA), to further enhance performance, as demonstrated in wireless sensor networks for intrusion detection. By selecting only the most relevant features, GAs reduce computational overhead and improve real-time detection capabilities. This optimization not only enhances classification accuracy but also minimizes false positives, making genetic algorithm-based feature selection a powerful tool for modern IDS in environments like IoT botnet detection and industrial control systems.

4.1.5 Key Benefits of Using Genetic Algorithms in Feature Selection for Nids

Genetic algorithms (GAs) offer several key benefits in feature selection for Network Intrusion Detection Systems (NIDS). First, they effectively reduce data dimensionality by identifying the most relevant features, which minimizes noise and redundant information, thereby improving the accuracy and interpretability of detection models. This optimization ensures that NIDS can focus on critical attributes, enhancing its ability to identify intrusions with higher precision.

Second, GAs adaptively explore the feature space using evolutionary techniques such as selection, crossover, and mutation, ensuring robust solutions even in high-dimensional datasets. This adaptability allows NIDS to dynamically adjust to evolving attack patterns and diverse network conditions. Additionally, GAs improve computational efficiency by selecting smaller subsets of features, which reduces processing overhead and enables real-time intrusion detection in complex environments. These advantages make genetic algorithms a powerful tool for optimizing feature selection in NIDS.

Video Resources
https://www.youtube.com/watch?v=RuhNpsRZHcU

Use of ICT

The use of Information and Communication Technology (ICT) for integrating fuzzy logic and genetic algorithms in Intrusion Detection Systems (IDS) enhances the adaptability and accuracy of detecting complex cyber threats. ICT enables the application of fuzzy data mining techniques to analyze ambiguous or overlapping data patterns, improving anomaly detection by identifying deviations from normal behavior. Genetic algorithms, supported by ICT infrastructure, optimize fuzzy membership functions and feature selection, ensuring efficient and scalable IDS deployment in dynamic network environments. ICT also facilitates the processing of large datasets, such as KDD'99, enabling the development of hybrid IDS models that combine fuzzy logic's interpretability with genetic algorithms' optimization capabilities for superior intrusion detection performance. By leveraging ICT resources, these advanced IDS frameworks provide robust solutions for addressing evolving cybersecurity challenges in modern networks.

4.2 HYBRID IDS MODELS COMBINING SIGNATURE-BASED AND ANOMALY-BASED METHODS

Hybrid IDS models represent a strategic approach to network security by integrating the strengths of both signature-based and anomaly-based detection methods. Signature-based detection excels at identifying known threats by matching network traffic against a database of predefined attack signatures.

However, it struggles to detect novel or zero-day exploits. Anomaly-based detection, on the other hand, uses machine learning algorithms to establish a baseline of normal network behavior and flags deviations from this baseline as potential threats. This makes it effective at detecting unknown attacks, but it can also generate false positives due to legitimate, yet unusual, network activity. By combining these approaches, hybrid IDS models aim to provide comprehensive threat coverage, reducing both false negatives (missed attacks) and false positives (incorrect alerts).

The implementation of hybrid IDS as given in figure 4.3 often involves a multi-layered architecture where signature-based detection acts as the first line of defense, quickly identifying and blocking known threats. Traffic that does not match any known signatures is then passed to the anomaly detection engine for further analysis. Machine learning techniques, such as K-Means clustering, Isolation Forests, or deep learning models like CNNs and LSTMs, can be used to detect subtle anomalies in network traffic patterns. The integration of Information and Communication Technology (ICT) facilitates the real-time processing and analysis of large-scale data, enabling these models to adapt to evolving threats and maintain high detection accuracy. This hybrid approach leverages the speed and precision of signature-based detection with the adaptability and broad coverage of anomaly-based detection to create a more robust and effective IDS.

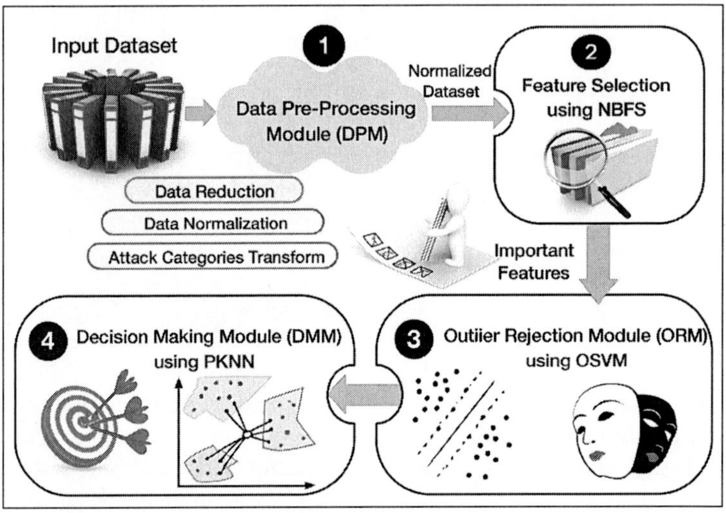

Figure 4.3: Hybrid IDS

4.2.1 What are the Computational Requirements for Implementing Hybrid IDS Models

The computational requirements for implementing hybrid Intrusion Detection Systems (IDS) are influenced by their need to combine multiple detection methods, such as signature-based and anomaly-based techniques, often enhanced with machine learning or deep learning algorithms. Below are the key computational demands.

- **High Processing Power**: Hybrid IDS models require significant processing power to handle the simultaneous execution of signature-based and anomaly-based detection methods. Machine learning algorithms like Support Vector Machines (SVM), Decision Trees, or deep learning techniques such as CNNs and GRUs demand robust computational resources for training and inference, especially when analyzing large-scale network traffic data.
- **Memory Requirements**: These systems need substantial memory to store attack signatures, normal behavior profiles, and intermediate data during feature extraction and classification. For instance, deep learning models like CNN-GRU require memory for both model parameters and input data during training and real-time detection.
- **Data Preprocessing and Feature Optimization**: Preprocessing large datasets and optimizing features are computationally intensive tasks. Techniques like Multi-Objective Evolutionary Feature Selection (MOEFS) are used to reduce dimensionality while retaining critical features, which requires both CPU and GPU resources.

- **Real-Time Analysis**: Hybrid IDS must process network traffic in real-time to detect intrusions promptly. This necessitates fast hardware like GPUs or TPUs to accelerate computations, particularly for deep learning-based anomaly detection models.
- **Scalability**: To handle increasing network sizes and traffic volumes, hybrid IDS must scale efficiently. This involves distributed computing environments or cloud-based solutions that can manage large-scale data streams while maintaining performance.
- **Storage Requirements**: Hybrid IDS models require storage for datasets used in training, testing, and updating attack signatures or behavioral profiles. Additionally, logs of detected threats are stored for analysis and auditing purposes.

4.2.2 How do Hybrid IDS Models Improve Detection Accuracy Compared to Single-Method IDS

Hybrid Intrusion Detection Systems (IDS) improve detection accuracy by leveraging the strengths of both signature-based and anomaly-based methods. Signature-based detection excels at identifying known attacks by comparing network activity against a database of predefined attack patterns, ensuring high precision for familiar threats. However, it struggles to detect novel or zero-day attacks. Anomaly-based detection complements this by identifying deviations from normal network behavior, which helps to uncover previously unknown threats. By combining these two approaches, hybrid IDS models reduce the likelihood of false negatives (missed attacks) while maintaining a low rate of false positives (incorrect alerts), thereby enhancing overall detection accuracy.

For example, hybrid models often employ multi-stage architectures where signature-based methods act as the first layer of defense, quickly filtering out known threats. Anomaly-based methods then analyze the remaining traffic for unusual patterns using advanced techniques like machine learning or ensemble models. Studies have demonstrated that such hybrid systems achieve superior results compared to single-method IDS. For instance, one hybrid model using convolutional and LSTM networks achieved a detection accuracy of 97.29%, outperforming traditional machine learning approaches1. Another hybrid IDS designed for IoT networks achieved an impressive 99.97% accuracy by combining C5 classifiers and one-class SVMs in a layered architecture2. These examples highlight how hybrid IDS models optimize detection performance while addressing the limitations of individual methods.

4.2.3 What are the Key Challenges in Implementing Hybrid IDS Models in Different Environments

Implementing hybrid Intrusion Detection Systems (IDS) in different environments comes with several challenges, which can vary depending on the specific context, such as hybrid networks, cloud environments, or IoT systems. Below are the key challenges:

Interoperability and Integration

- ✓ Combining multiple detection techniques (e.g., signature-based and anomaly-based) within a single system can be difficult due to differences in their underlying mechanisms. Ensuring seamless interoperability between these methods is a significant challenge.

- ✓ In hybrid environments, integrating IDS with existing security frameworks like Security Information and Event Management (SIEM) systems requires careful configuration to avoid compatibility issues.

Scalability and Performance

- ✓ Hybrid IDSs must process large volumes of network data in real time, which can strain computational resources. This challenge is especially pronounced in hybrid cloud or IoT environments where data flows are highly dynamic and distributed.
- ✓ Ensuring low latency while maintaining high detection accuracy is critical but computationally demanding, particularly when using machine learning models.

False Positives and Class Imbalance

- ✓ Anomaly-based components of hybrid IDSs often generate high false-positive rates, which can overwhelm security teams with unnecessary alerts.
- ✓ Class imbalance in training datasets—where attack instances are far fewer than normal traffic—can reduce the effectiveness of machine learning models used in hybrid IDSs.

Feature Selection and Model Optimization

- ✓ Selecting the most relevant features for detection models is computationally intensive but crucial for improving accuracy. Techniques like Multi-Objective Evolutionary Feature Selection (MOEFS) are often required but add complexity to implementation.
- ✓ Optimizing machine learning models for diverse environments requires extensive tuning, which can be resource-intensive.

Security and Privacy Concerns

- ✓ In hybrid networks, securing sensitive data across on-premises and cloud infrastructures is challenging due to varying security policies and compliance requirements. Insecure APIs and lack of visibility exacerbate these risks.
- ✓ Privacy-preserving methods must be incorporated into anomaly detection models to ensure that sensitive user data is not exposed during analysis.

Video Resources
https://www.mdpi.com/2079-9292/8/11/1210

Use of ICT

Hybrid Intrusion Detection Systems (IDS) combining signature-based and anomaly-based methods leverage Information and Communication Technology (ICT) to enhance security through integrated detection mechanisms. ICT applications include advanced computational frameworks like distributed computing and big data tools such as Apache Spark, which enable real-time processing and scalable analysis of network data. Machine learning and AI play a crucial role with ensemble models like C5 decision trees combined with one-class SVM achieving high accuracy rates, and deep learning techniques such as Convolutional-LSTM networks analyzing sequential traffic patterns. Feature engineering involves optimizing feature selection using information gain principles and dynamic reduction techniques to improve detection accuracy. Protocol and traffic analysis modules monitor specific protocols and packet content to identify known threats while anomaly detection flags unknown exploits. Overall, ICT-driven hybrid IDS systems offer high accuracy, scalability, and adaptability, making them effective for securing both IoT and enterprise networks.

4.3 DISTRIBUTED IDS FOR LARGE-SCALE NETWORKS

Distributed IDS are crucial for monitoring extensive and complex networks by distributing detection tasks across multiple nodes. In large-scale networks, a centralized IDS can become a bottleneck, struggling to process vast amounts of data in real-time. A distributed architecture allows for localized monitoring and analysis, reducing latency and improving scalability. Each node in the distributed IDS monitors a specific segment of the network, analyzing traffic for anomalies and known threats. This approach enhances the ability to detect and respond to intrusions promptly, especially in dynamic environments such as cloud computing and IoT networks.

The implementation of a distributed IDS involves several key components, including sensors, analysis engines, and a central management system. Sensors are deployed throughout the network to capture traffic data, which is then analyzed locally by analysis engines using techniques like machine learning and deep learning. These engines can employ anomaly detection algorithms like K-Means clustering, Isolation Forests, or deep learning models such as CNNs and LSTMs to identify suspicious activities. The central management system aggregates alerts from the distributed nodes, provides a unified view of the network security posture, and coordinates response actions. Effective use of Information and Communication Technology (ICT) infrastructure is essential for seamless data collection, processing, and communication between the distributed components, ensuring robust and adaptive security across the entire network.

Video Resources
https://pmc.ncbi.nlm.nih.gov/articles/PMC9259256/

Use of ICT

The use of Information and Communication Technology (ICT) for Distributed Intrusion Detection Systems (DIDS) in large-scale networks focuses on leveraging advanced technologies to enhance security, scalability, and real-time threat detection. ICT enables the deployment of distributed IDS across multiple nodes, where each node monitors specific segments of the network and communicates with a centralized server for orchestration. Big data tools like Apache Spark facilitate the processing of massive volumes of network traffic, while machine learning algorithms, including transfer learning and deep learning models like CNN-LSTM, improve anomaly detection and classification accuracy. Multi-access edge computing (MEC) further enhances DIDS by enabling localized processing near data sources, reducing latency and improving responsiveness. These systems also utilize signature-based methods for identifying known threats and anomaly-based techniques for detecting zero-day attacks. By integrating dynamic feature extraction, cooperative information exchange, and context-awareness modules, ICT-driven DIDS provide robust defense mechanisms against internal and external cyber threats in IoT environments and industrial control systems.

4.4 INTRUSION RESPONSE AND ALERT CORRELATION SYSTEMS

Intrusion response and alert correlation systems as given in figure 4.4 are critical components of modern cybersecurity infrastructure, designed to manage and mitigate the impact of detected intrusions effectively. These systems aggregate and analyze security alerts from various sources, such as Intrusion Detection Systems (IDS), firewalls, and endpoint protection tools, to identify and prioritize genuine threats. By correlating alerts, they reduce false positives and provide a comprehensive view of ongoing attacks, enabling security teams to understand the scope and severity of incidents. Effective intrusion response involves automated actions, such as quarantining infected systems, blocking malicious traffic, and notifying relevant personnel, to minimize damage and prevent further spread of the attack.

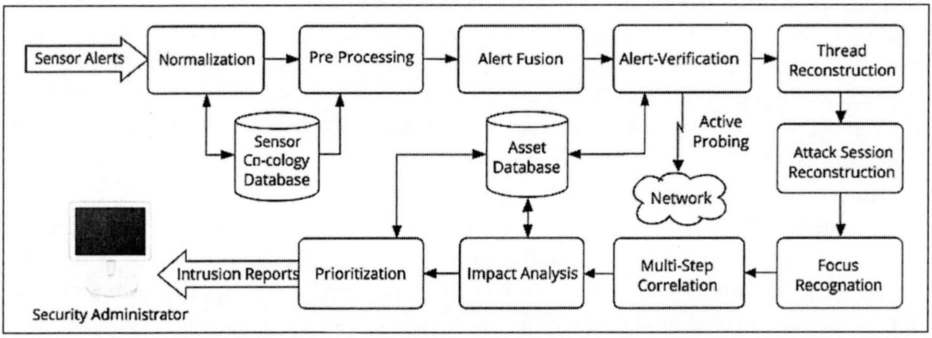

Figure 4.4: *Intrusion Detection Alert Correlation*

Alert correlation is often achieved through advanced techniques like machine learning, which can identify patterns and relationships between seemingly disparate events. For example, machine learning algorithms can analyze network traffic data, system logs, and user activity to detect coordinated attacks or zero-day exploits that might be missed by traditional signature-based methods.

Additionally, the use of Information and Communication Technology (ICT) facilitates real-time data processing and analysis, enabling rapid response to emerging threats. By integrating these technologies, intrusion response and alert correlation systems enhance an organization's ability to detect, analyze, and respond to security incidents, thereby improving overall cybersecurity posture.

Video Resources
https://www.mdpi.com/1999-4893/10/2/39

Use of ICT

Intrusion Response and Alert Correlation Systems utilize Information and Communication Technology (ICT) to enhance threat detection, automate responses, and streamline security operations. These systems integrate signature-based and anomaly-based detection methods to reduce false positives and improve accuracy. ICT facilitates real-time monitoring through Network Intrusion Detection Systems (NIDS) and Host-based IDS (HIDS), analyzing traffic at various layers to detect threats like SQL injections. Alert correlation relies on centralized platforms such as Security Information and Event Management (SIEM) tools, which aggregate data from distributed sensors to identify multi-stage attack patterns. Advanced ICT frameworks employ machine learning to prioritize alerts, enabling faster incident response. Automated actions are triggered through Intrusion Prevention Systems (IPS), blocking malicious IPs or isolating compromised devices. This proactive approach mitigates threats like DDoS attacks or ransomware, maintaining compliance with regulations while enhancing resilience against zero-day exploits through hybrid detection models.

4.5 REAL-TIME IDS WITH BIG DATA ANALYTICS

Real-time Intrusion Detection Systems (IDS) as shown in figure 4.5 have evolved to leverage big data analytics to address the challenges posed by modern, large-scale networks. Traditional IDS methods often struggle with the volume, velocity, and variety of data generated in contemporary network environments, leading to delayed detection and increased false positives. By integrating big data analytics, real-time IDS can efficiently process and analyze vast datasets, identifying subtle patterns and anomalies that indicate potential security threats. This approach enables rapid threat detection and response, crucial for maintaining network integrity and minimizing potential damage from cyberattacks.

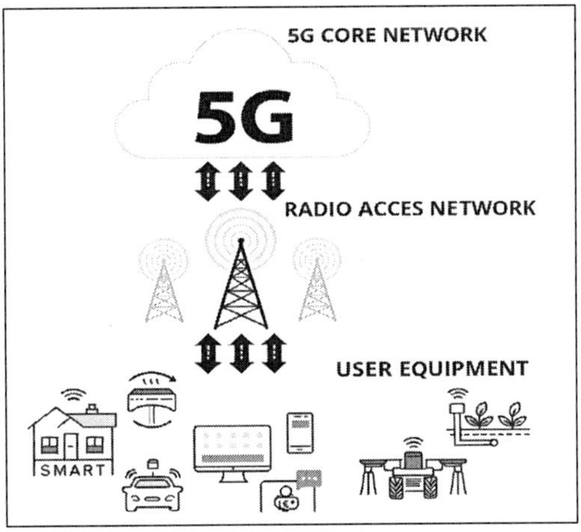

Figure 4.5: Real time Intrusion Detection

The implementation of real-time IDS with big data analytics involves several key technologies and techniques. Big data platforms like Apache Hadoop and Apache Spark provide the infrastructure for storing and processing large volumes of network traffic data. Machine learning algorithms, including both supervised and unsupervised methods, are employed to detect anomalies and classify threats. Deep learning architectures such as Convolutional Neural Networks (CNNs) and Long Short-Term Memory (LSTM) networks can automatically learn complex patterns from raw data, enhancing detection accuracy. Feature engineering and dataset preparation are also critical, involving techniques like density-based clustering and feature selection algorithms to optimize model performance and reduce computational overhead.

The integration of Information and Communication Technology (ICT) is essential for the success of real-time IDS with big data analytics. ICT infrastructure facilitates the collection of data from diverse sources, including network logs, IoT devices, and cloud services. Real-time data processing is enabled through ICT systems that integrate machine learning algorithms into platforms like cloud services or edge devices. Additionally, cloud-based ICT platforms allow for scalable deployment of anomaly detection models, supporting continuous learning by updating models with new data. This holistic approach empowers organizations to enhance their cybersecurity posture, enabling timely detection and mitigation of threats in dynamic and complex network environments.

Video Resources
https://www.youtube.com/watch?v=OS9xRGKfx4E

Use of ICT

For the topic of Real-time IDS with big data analytics, the use of Information and Communication Technology (ICT) is pivotal in enabling the collection, processing, and analysis of massive datasets required for effective intrusion detection. ICT infrastructure facilitates the integration of diverse data sources, including network logs, security events, and user activity, into a unified platform. Real-time data processing is achieved through high-performance computing systems, cloud services, and edge computing devices, which employ machine learning and deep learning algorithms to identify anomalies and detect potential threats. ICT tools also provide visualization interfaces and reporting mechanisms, enabling security analysts to interpret detected anomalies, assess their severity, and implement appropriate response measures in a timely manner, thereby enhancing overall network security.

4.6 CASE STUDY: SECURENET TECHNOLOGIES – IMPLEMENTING ADVANCED IDS TECHNIQUES IN A FINANCIAL INSTITUTION

Here, we can use the information about machine learning and deep learning in IDS to create a plausible scenario for a financial institution.

4.6.1 The Challenge

Financial institutions face relentless cyber threats, ranging from sophisticated phishing attacks to advanced persistent threats (APTs) targeting sensitive financial data. Traditional signature-based Intrusion Detection Systems (IDS) often fall short in detecting novel or zero-day exploits, leaving institutions vulnerable. SecureNet Technologies, a leading cybersecurity firm, was approached by a major financial institution to enhance its security posture by implementing advanced IDS techniques capable of detecting and responding to evolving threats in real-time. The goal was to move beyond reactive security measures and establish a proactive defense mechanism that could adapt to new attack vectors.

4.6.2 The Solution - A Hybrid Approach

SecureNet Technologies proposed a hybrid IDS solution that combined the strengths of both signature-based and anomaly-based detection methods, enhanced with machine learning (ML) and deep learning (DL) algorithms. The solution involved deploying network sensors to capture traffic data, which was then processed by a combination of traditional signature-based IDS and advanced anomaly detection engines. For anomaly detection, machine learning models like Isolation Forests and K-Means clustering were used to identify deviations from normal network behavior. More complex threat patterns were identified using deep learning architectures, such as Recurrent Neural Networks (RNNs) and Long Short-Term Memory (LSTM) networks, which are adept at analyzing time-series data.

4.6.3 Implementation and Feature Engineering

The implementation involved significant feature engineering and dataset preparation to optimize the performance of the machine learning models. SecureNet Technologies employed techniques like density-based clustering to address class imbalance issues, where attack instances were far fewer than normal traffic. They also used feature selection algorithms to identify the most relevant network traffic features, reducing computational overhead and improving detection accuracy. The models were trained using both labeled and unlabeled data, leveraging semi-supervised learning techniques to maximize the use of available data and improve generalization.

4.6.4 Results and Performance

The hybrid IDS demonstrated significantly improved detection accuracy compared to the institution's previous signature-based system. The anomaly-based detection component was particularly effective in identifying previously unknown attacks and insider threats. The deep learning models, such as LSTM networks, proved capable of detecting complex attack patterns that spanned extended periods. Furthermore, the system's real-time processing capabilities, facilitated by cloud-based ICT infrastructure, enabled rapid response to emerging threats, reducing the potential impact of successful intrusions. The financial institution observed a significant reduction in false positives, allowing their security team to focus on genuine threats.

4.6.5 Future Directions

The successful implementation of advanced IDS techniques at the financial institution highlighted the importance of a multi-layered security approach that combines traditional and modern methods. The project underscored the need for continuous monitoring, model retraining, and adaptation to evolving threat landscapes. SecureNet Technologies plans to further enhance the system by incorporating federated learning techniques to improve model generalization across multiple financial institutions while preserving data privacy. They also aim to explore explainable AI (XAI) methods to provide greater transparency into the decision-making processes of the deep learning models, facilitating trust and acceptance among security personnel.

Video Resources
https://www.youtube.com/watch?v=OS9xRGKfx4E

Use of ICT

SecureNet Technologies leveraged Information and Communication Technology (ICT) extensively to deploy advanced IDS techniques within the financial institution. ICT infrastructure facilitated the collection of network traffic data from various sources, which was then processed by machine learning and deep learning algorithms hosted on cloud-based platforms. The use of high-performance computing resources, including GPUs, accelerated the training of complex models like LSTMs, enabling real-time anomaly detection. ICT also supported secure communication channels for transmitting alerts and coordinating responses, ensuring that security personnel could rapidly address emerging threats. Furthermore, cloud-based ICT allowed for scalable deployment of the IDS, enabling it to adapt to the evolving needs of the financial institution while maintaining high availability and performance.

SUMMARY

- **Fuzzy Logic and Genetic Algorithms in IDS**: These techniques are used to enhance intrusion detection by improving adaptability, reducing false positives, and handling ambiguous or complex attack patterns effectively.
- **Hybrid IDS Models**: Combining signature-based and anomaly-based methods leverages the strengths of both approaches, enabling the detection of known attacks while identifying novel threats.

- **Distributed IDS for Large-Scale Networks**: Distributed systems ensure scalability and efficient monitoring of large, complex networks by decentralizing detection processes.
- **Intrusion Response and Alert Correlation Systems**: Advanced systems improve decision-making by correlating alerts from multiple sources, reducing false alarms, and enabling faster responses to threats.
- **Real-Time IDS with Big Data Analytics**: Leveraging big data analytics allows real-time processing of vast datasets, enhancing the speed and accuracy of intrusion detection in dynamic environments.

EXERCISES

A. Subjective Questions

Category-I *(Revised Bloom's Levels-1, 2 & 3)*

1. Define fuzzy logic and explain its role in enhancing IDS performance.
2. Describe the benefits of combining signature-based and anomaly-based methods in hybrid IDS models.
3. Explain the concept of distributed IDS and its importance in large-scale networks.
4. What are intrusion response systems, and how do they correlate alerts to improve detection accuracy?
5. Summarize the key features of real-time IDS with big data analytics for modern cybersecurity challenges.

Category-II *(Revised Bloom's Levels-4, 5 & 6)*

1. Analyze the advantages and limitations of using genetic algorithms in IDS for optimizing threat detection.
2. Design a hybrid IDS model that combines signature-based and anomaly-based techniques for a financial institution's network security.
3. Evaluate the scalability and efficiency of distributed IDS in high-speed networks using real-world examples.
4. Propose an alert correlation strategy to reduce false positives in intrusion detection systems for large-scale enterprises.
5. Critically assess the role of big data analytics in enabling real-time intrusion detection and suggest improvements for future implementations.

B. Objective Questions

Category-I *(Revised Bloom's Levels-1, 2 & 3)*

1. What is the primary purpose of fuzzy logic in IDS?
   (a) To create attack signatures
   (b) To handle uncertainty in decision-making
   (c) To improve network throughput
   (d) To encrypt sensitive data

2. Which method is NOT a feature of hybrid IDS models?
   (a) Signature-based detection
   (b) Anomaly-based detection
   (c) Predictive analytics
   (d) Static rule enforcement
3. What is a key advantage of distributed IDS?
   (a) Centralized monitoring system
   (b) Scalability for large networks
   (c) Reduced computational overhead
   (d) Elimination of false positives
4. Alert correlation systems are primarily used to:
   (a) Generate attack signatures automatically
   (b) Combine and analyze alerts from multiple sources
   (c) Encrypt network traffic for secure communication
   (d) Reduce network latency during analysis
5. Big data analytics in real-time IDS helps to:
   (a) Process large datasets quickly for timely threat detection
   (b) Replace traditional anomaly detection methods entirely
   (c) Store historical data for forensic analysis only
   (d) Simplify network configurations

Ans.: 1. (b), 2. (b), 3. (b), 4. (b), 5. (a)

Category-II *(Revised Bloom's Levels-4, 5 & 6)*

1. Which scenario best demonstrates the use of genetic algorithms in IDS?
   (a) Developing static rules for known threats
   (b) Optimizing feature selection for anomaly detection
   (c) Encrypting sensitive network traffic
   (d) Generating predefined attack signatures
2. What is the most significant challenge in implementing distributed IDS?
   (a) Handling high volumes of alerts efficiently
   (b) Lack of computational power at endpoints
   (c) Inability to detect unknown threats
   (d) Difficulty in creating attack signatures
3. Which component is essential for real-time IDS with big data analytics?
   (a) Static rule-based systems
   (b) High-speed data processing frameworks like Apache Spark
   (c) Centralized monitoring servers
   (d) Predefined alert thresholds
4. Hybrid IDS models are effective because they:
   (a) Focus solely on known threats
   (b) Combine multiple detection techniques to address diverse threats
   (c) Eliminate the need for anomaly detection entirely
   (d) Use only signature-based methods for faster processing

5. How does SecureNet Technologies implement advanced IDS techniques in financial institutions? *(Open-ended MCQ with justification)*

Ans.: 1. (b), 2. (a), 3. (b), 4. (b)

TEACHER'S KNOW MORE

To effectively teach the topics in this chapter, educators should focus on advanced techniques and hybrid models in Intrusion Detection Systems (IDS), which combine innovative methods to address modern cybersecurity challenges. Fuzzy logic and genetic algorithms enhance IDS adaptability and accuracy by handling ambiguous attack patterns, while hybrid models integrate signature-based and anomaly-based approaches to detect both known and unknown threats effectively. Distributed IDS are emphasized for their scalability in large-scale networks, enabling efficient monitoring of complex environments. Intrusion response and alert correlation systems are critical for reducing false positives and improving real-time decision-making. The integration of big data analytics into IDS allows for the processing of vast datasets, enabling real-time detection of sophisticated threats. The case study on "SecureNet Technologies" provides practical insights into implementing these advanced techniques in financial institutions, showcasing their effectiveness in securing critical infrastructures against evolving cyber threats.

Future Trends and Research Challenges

5

UNIT

RATIONALE

This chapter examines the future trends and research challenges in Intrusion Detection Systems (IDS), addressing the evolving landscape of cybersecurity threats and innovative solutions. It begins by exploring emerging cyber threats and expanding attack surfaces, emphasizing the need for adaptive IDS to counter sophisticated adversarial techniques like machine learning attacks. The integration of IDS with Security Information and Event Management (SIEM) systems is highlighted as a critical step toward comprehensive threat detection and response. Autonomous and self-healing IDS are introduced, showcasing their ability to proactively adapt and recover from attacks without manual intervention. Open research challenges, such as improving scalability, reducing false positives, and developing robust models against adversarial attacks, are discussed to inspire future advancements. The case study on protecting smart city infrastructure demonstrates practical applications of advanced IDS techniques, providing insights into securing complex systems against dynamic threats while paving the way for innovative research directions.

OUTCOMES

- **Understand Emerging Cyber Threats**: Students will understand emerging cyber threats and evolving attack surfaces to better prepare for sophisticated adversarial techniques.
- **Analyze Adversarial Attacks on IDS**: They will analyze how adversarial machine learning attacks impact IDS and explore strategies to mitigate these threats.
- **Integrate IDS with SIEM Systems**: Integrating IDS with Security Information and Event Management (SIEM) systems will be covered to enhance comprehensive threat detection and response.
- **Explore Autonomous and Self-Healing IDS**: Students will explore the principles of autonomous and self-healing IDS that can adaptively detect, respond to, and recover from cyberattacks.
- **Address Open Research Challenges**: Finally, they will address open research challenges in IDS development, proposing innovative solutions for securing complex infrastructures like smart cities.

5.1 EMERGING CYBER THREATS AND EVOLVING ATTACK SURFACES

The landscape of cyber threats is constantly evolving, presenting new challenges for network security. Emerging threats include sophisticated ransomware attacks, supply chain compromises, and state-sponsored espionage campaigns. Attackers are increasingly leveraging advanced techniques such as artificial intelligence (AI) and machine learning (ML) to automate and scale their operations, making them more difficult to detect. The expanding attack surface, driven by the proliferation of IoT devices, cloud computing, and remote work environments, further complicates the task of maintaining robust security. Organizations must adapt their security strategies to address these dynamic threats and protect their critical assets.

Evolving attack surfaces are characterized by an increase in interconnected systems and devices, creating numerous entry points for malicious actors. The rise of cloud computing has led to a more distributed IT infrastructure, with data and applications spread across multiple environments. IoT devices, often lacking robust security measures, add further complexity and vulnerability. Cybercriminals exploit these weaknesses to launch a variety of attacks, including data breaches, malware infections, and denial-of-service attacks. Effective security measures must encompass all aspects of the evolving attack surface, from endpoint protection to network segmentation and cloud security.

Addressing these challenges requires a proactive and adaptive approach to cybersecurity. Organizations should prioritize threat intelligence to stay informed about the latest attack techniques and vulnerabilities. Implementing robust security controls, such as multi-factor authentication, intrusion detection systems, and security information and event management (SIEM) solutions, is essential. Furthermore, continuous monitoring, incident response planning, and regular security audits are crucial for detecting and responding to cyber threats effectively. By embracing a comprehensive security strategy, organizations can mitigate the risks posed by emerging cyber threats and protect their digital assets.

Video Resources
https://www.youtube.com/watch?v=W6VTEd5jHlc

Use of ICT

To address emerging cyber threats and evolving attack surfaces effectively, Information and Communication Technology (ICT) plays a crucial role in enabling advanced security measures. ICT infrastructure facilitates the collection and analysis of vast amounts of data from diverse sources, including network logs, IoT devices, and cloud services, providing comprehensive visibility into potential threats. Technologies such as cloud computing, machine learning, and artificial intelligence are leveraged to develop adaptive security solutions that can detect and respond to evolving attack patterns in real-time. Furthermore, ICT enables secure communication channels for sharing threat intelligence and coordinating incident response efforts across distributed teams, ensuring a unified and proactive approach to cybersecurity.

5.2 ADVERSARIAL MACHINE LEARNING ATTACKS ON IDS

5.2.1 The Vulnerability of Machine Learning-Based IDS

Machine learning (ML) and deep learning (DL) have revolutionized Intrusion Detection Systems (IDS), enhancing their ability to detect complex and evolving cyber threats. However, these models are not immune to attacks. Adversarial machine learning introduces a new dimension to cybersecurity, where malicious actors craft specific inputs designed to fool ML-based IDS. These attacks exploit the inherent vulnerabilities of ML algorithms, causing them to misclassify malicious traffic as benign, thereby allowing intrusions to go undetected. This emerging threat necessitates a deeper understanding of adversarial techniques and the development of robust defense mechanisms.

5.2.2 Types of Adversarial Attacks on IDS

Adversarial attacks on IDS can be broadly categorized into evasion attacks, poisoning attacks, and exploratory attacks. Evasion attacks occur during the testing or deployment phase, where attackers carefully modify malicious samples to evade detection without altering their underlying functionality. Poisoning attacks involve injecting malicious data into the training dataset, corrupting the model's learning process and causing it to misclassify future inputs. Exploratory attacks aim to probe the model's decision boundaries to gain insights into its weaknesses, enabling the development of more effective evasion strategies. Each type of attack poses a unique challenge and requires tailored defense strategies.

5.2.3 Example of an Evasion Attack

Consider a scenario where an attacker modifies a malicious network packet by adding small, imperceptible changes to its features. These changes, carefully crafted using techniques like gradient-based optimization, are designed to minimize the model's confidence in classifying the packet as malicious. The modified packet retains its malicious payload but is now classified as benign by the IDS, allowing it to bypass security controls and compromise the targeted system. This example highlights the potential impact of evasion attacks and the need for robust defense mechanisms that can detect subtle adversarial perturbations. The evasion attack is as given in figure 5.1.

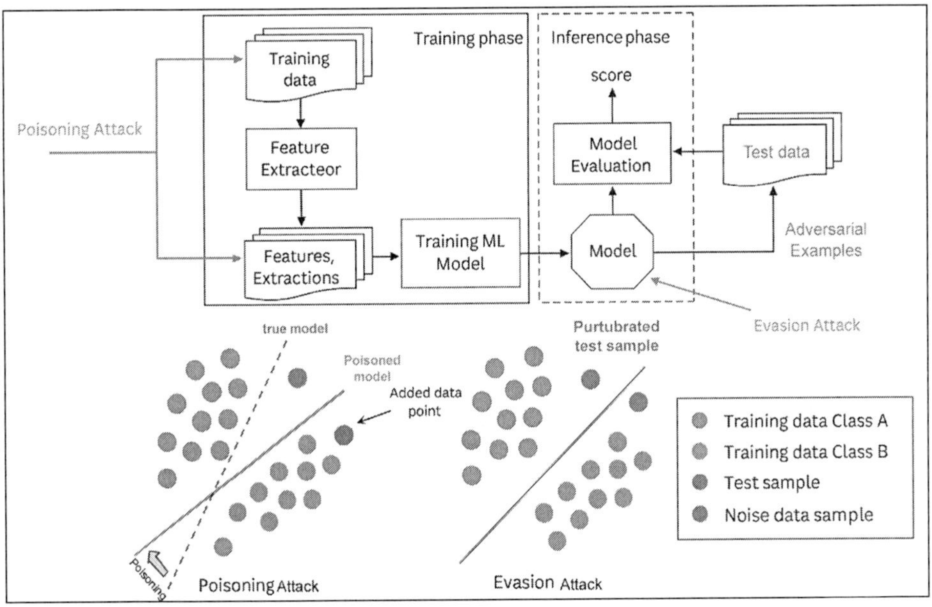

Figure 5.1: Evasion attack

5.2.4 Defenses Against Adversarial Attacks

Mitigating adversarial attacks on IDS requires a multi-faceted approach that includes robust model training, input validation, and adversarial detection techniques. Adversarial training involves augmenting the training dataset with adversarially perturbed samples, forcing the model to learn to recognize and classify these inputs correctly. Input validation techniques, such as feature sanitization and anomaly detection, can help identify and filter out potentially malicious inputs. Additionally, adversarial detection methods can be employed to detect when an input is likely to be an adversarial example, triggering additional security measures. By implementing these defenses, organizations can enhance the resilience of their IDS against adversarial attacks and maintain a strong security posture.

Video Resources
https://www.youtube.com/watch?v=W6VTEd5jHlc

Use of ICT

To effectively counter adversarial machine learning attacks on Intrusion Detection Systems (IDS), Information and Communication Technology (ICT) plays a crucial role in enabling proactive defense mechanisms. ICT infrastructure facilitates the development and deployment of advanced machine learning models capable of detecting subtle adversarial perturbations in network traffic data. By leveraging cloud-based platforms and high-performance computing resources, security professionals can train robust models using techniques like adversarial training and input validation to enhance the resilience of IDS against evolving attack strategies.

Furthermore, ICT enables real-time monitoring and analysis of network traffic, allowing for the prompt identification and mitigation of adversarial attacks, thereby ensuring a strong and adaptive cybersecurity posture.

5.3 INTEGRATING IDS WITH SIEM (SECURITY INFORMATION AND EVENT MANAGEMENT)

5.3.1 Enhancing Threat Detection with Integrated Systems

Integrating Intrusion Detection Systems (IDS) with Security Information and Event Management (SIEM) systems is crucial for enhancing threat detection and incident response capabilities. IDS solutions monitor network traffic for malicious activity, generating alerts when suspicious behavior is detected.

However, these alerts often lack context and can result in a high volume of false positives, overwhelming security teams. SIEM systems, on the other hand, aggregate and analyze security data from various sources across the IT infrastructure, providing a centralized platform for threat analysis and incident management. By integrating IDS with SIEM, organizations can correlate IDS alerts with other security events, gaining a more comprehensive understanding of potential threats and prioritizing incidents for investigation.

5.3.2 Alert Correlation and Contextualization

The key benefit of integrating IDS with SIEM as given in figure 5.2, is the ability to perform alert correlation and contextualization. SIEM systems can analyze IDS alerts in conjunction with logs from firewalls, servers, and other security devices to identify patterns and relationships between events. For example, a SIEM system might correlate an IDS alert indicating a potential SQL injection attack with a web server log showing unusual database access attempts, confirming a successful intrusion. This contextual information enables security teams to distinguish between legitimate security incidents and false positives, reducing alert fatigue and improving incident response efficiency.

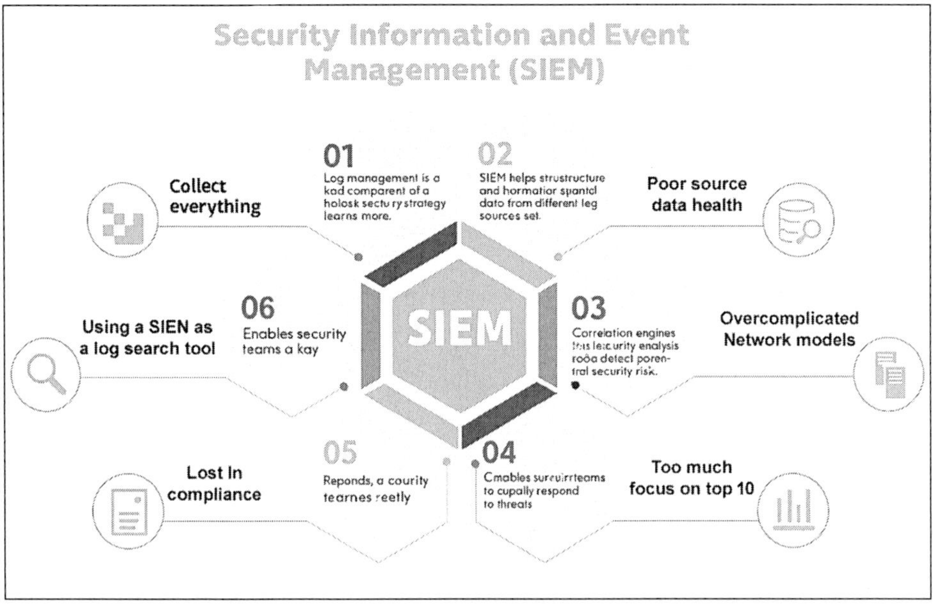

Figure 5.2: *SIEM*

5.3.3 Automation and Response Orchestration

Beyond alert correlation, integrating IDS with SIEM enables automation and response orchestration. SIEM systems can be configured to automatically trigger predefined actions in response to specific security events. For instance, if an IDS detects a malware infection, the SIEM system can automatically isolate the affected system, block malicious traffic, and notify the security team. This automation streamlines incident response processes, reducing the time it takes to contain and remediate security incidents. Additionally, the integration allows for continuous monitoring and analysis of security data, providing valuable insights into the organization's security posture and enabling proactive threat hunting.

5.3.4 Python Program: Basic Alert Correlation

This Python program demonstrates a very basic alert correlation between IDS and firewall logs. It simulates receiving alerts from both systems and identifies potential matches based on IP addresses.

```
python
import json
# Sample IDS alerts (simulated)
ids_alerts = [
{"timestamp": "2024-03-16 10:00:00", "src_ip": "192.168.1.100", "alert_type": "SQL Injection"},
{"timestamp": "2024-03-16 10:05:00", "src_ip": "192.168.1.101", "alert_type": "Malware Infection"},
{"timestamp": "2024-03-16 10:10:00", "src_ip": "192.168.1.100", "alert_type": "Port Scan"}
]
# Sample Firewall logs (simulated)
```

```
firewall_logs = [
{"timestamp": "2024-03-16 10:00:05", "src_ip": "192.168.1.100", "action":
"Blocked", "protocol": "TCP", "port": 1433},
{"timestamp": "2024-03-16 10:05:10", "src_ip": "192.168.1.101", "action":
"Blocked", "protocol": "HTTP", "port": 80},
{"timestamp": "2024-03-16 10:15:00", "src_ip": "192.168.1.102", "action":
"Allowed", "protocol": "UDP", "port": 53}
]
# Function to correlate alerts based on IP address and timestamp
def correlate_alerts(ids_alerts, firewall_logs, time_window=60):
    correlated_alerts = []
    for ids_alert in ids_alerts:
        for firewall_log in firewall_logs:
            if ids_alert["src_ip"] == firewall_log["src_ip"]:
                time_diff = abs(
                            int(ids_alert["timestamp"].split(":")[1]) -
int(firewall_log["timestamp"].split(":")[1])
                )
                if time_diff <= time_window:
                    correlated_alerts.append({
                        "IDS Alert": ids_alert,
                        "Firewall Log": firewall_log
                    })
return correlated_alerts
# Correlate the alerts
correlated_events = correlate_alerts(ids_alerts, firewall_logs)
# Print the correlated events
print(json.dumps(correlated_events, indent=4))
```

Explanation

- ✓ **Simulated Data:** The code simulates IDS alerts and firewall logs as lists of dictionaries.
- ✓ **Correlation Function:** The `correlate_alerts` function takes the IDS alerts and firewall logs as input. It iterates through each IDS alert and compares the source IP address with the source IP address in the firewall logs. If the IP addresses match and the timestamps are within a defined `time_window` (60 seconds in this case), it considers them correlated and adds them to the `correlated_alerts` list.
- ✓ **Output:** The code prints the correlated events in JSON format.

Sample Output

```
json
 [
    {
        "IDS Alert": {
            "timestamp": "2024-03-16 10:00:00",
            "src_ip": "192.168.1.100",
```

```
            "alert_type": "SQL Injection"
        },
        "Firewall Log": {
            "timestamp": "2024-03-16 10:00:05",
            "src_ip": "192.168.1.100",
            "action": "Blocked",
            "protocol": "TCP",
            "port": 1433
        }
    },
    {
        "IDS Alert": {
            "timestamp": "2024-03-16 10:05:00",
            "src_ip": "192.168.1.101",
            "alert_type": "Malware Infection"
        },
        "Firewall Log": {
            "timestamp": "2024-03-16 10:05:10",
            "src_ip": "192.168.1.101",
            "action": "Blocked",
            "protocol": "HTTP",
            "port": 80
        }
    }
]
```

This output shows that the program has successfully correlated an IDS alert for a "SQL Injection" attack with a firewall log entry where traffic from the same IP address ("192.168.1.100") was blocked on port 1433 (commonly used for SQL Server). Similarly, it correlated a "Malware Infection" alert with a blocked HTTP connection from "192.168.1.101". This simple example illustrates how integrating IDS with SIEM can provide valuable context and enable more effective incident response.

Video Resources
https://www.youtube.com/watch?v=OS9xRGKfx4E

Use of ICT

The integration of Intrusion Detection Systems (IDS) with Security Information and Event Management (SIEM) systems leverages Information and Communication Technology (ICT) to create a powerful synergy for enhanced cybersecurity. ICT infrastructure facilitates the seamless collection, processing, and correlation of security data from diverse sources, including network logs, IoT devices, and cloud services, providing a comprehensive view of the threat landscape. Real-time data processing, enabled by high-performance computing systems and cloud-based platforms, allows for the prompt identification of suspicious activities and potential security breaches. Additionally, ICT tools offer visualization interfaces and reporting mechanisms that empower security analysts to interpret detected anomalies, assess their severity, and implement appropriate response measures in a timely manner, thereby strengthening the overall network security posture.

5.4 AUTONOMOUS AND SELF-HEALING IDS

5.4.1 The Need for Autonomy in Modern IDS

Traditional Intrusion Detection Systems (IDS) often rely on manual configuration, signature updates, and human intervention to identify and respond to security threats. However, the increasing complexity and velocity of modern cyberattacks necessitate more autonomous and self-healing systems. Autonomous IDS leverage machine learning (ML) and artificial intelligence (AI) to automatically adapt to changing network conditions, detect novel threats, and respond to incidents without human intervention. Self-healing capabilities enable the IDS to recover from failures, update security policies, and optimize performance based on real-time feedback, ensuring continuous and resilient protection. These advancements are critical for defending against sophisticated attacks in dynamic and distributed environments.

5.4.2 Core Components of Autonomous and Self-Healing IDS

An autonomous and self-healing IDS typically consists of several key components. First, an intelligent threat detection engine uses ML algorithms to identify anomalies, zero-day exploits, and advanced persistent threats (APTs). Second, an automated incident response module analyzes detected threats, determines the appropriate response actions, and executes them without human intervention. This may involve isolating infected systems, blocking malicious traffic, or updating firewall rules. Third, a self-healing mechanism continuously monitors the IDS components, detects failures, and automatically initiates recovery procedures, such as restarting services or reconfiguring network settings. Finally, a feedback loop collects data on the effectiveness of the IDS and uses it to retrain ML models, refine security policies, and optimize system performance. The self healing approach for IOT is as given in figure 5.3.

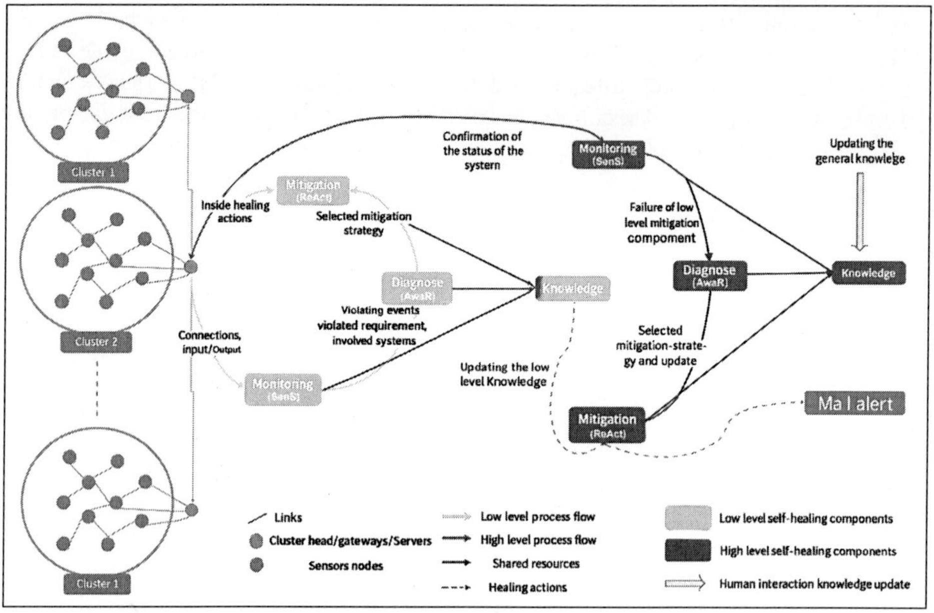

Figure 5.3: *Self Healing Approach in IOT*

5.4.3 Benefits and Challenges of Autonomous and Self-Healing IDS

Autonomous and self-healing IDS offer numerous benefits, including reduced reliance on human expertise, faster incident response times, improved detection accuracy, and enhanced resilience against evolving threats. However, these systems also face several challenges. Developing robust and reliable ML models requires large, high-quality datasets and careful feature engineering. Ensuring the security and integrity of the autonomous decision-making processes is crucial to prevent attackers from manipulating the IDS. Additionally, organizations must address ethical considerations related to automated responses and potential unintended consequences. Despite these challenges, the potential benefits of autonomous and self-healing IDS make them an essential component of modern cybersecurity strategies.

5.4.4 Python Program: Simulated Autonomous IDS with Anomaly Detection

This Python program simulates a simplified autonomous IDS that detects anomalies using K-Means clustering and automatically takes a mitigation action (simulated).

```
python
import numpy as np
import time
import random
from sklearn.cluster import KMeans
from sklearn.preprocessing import StandardScaler
import threading
# Configuration
NUM_FEATURES = 5
NUM_ANOMALIES = 5
TIME_WINDOW = 10 # Time window for anomaly detection
# Global variables
network_data = []
alert_status = False
def generate_network_data(num_samples=100):
    """Simulates network data (replace with real data source)."""
    data = np.random.rand(num_samples, NUM_FEATURES)
    # Inject some anomalies (high values in certain features)
    for _ in range(NUM_ANOMALIES):
        index = random.randint(0, num_samples - 1)
        feature_index = random.randint(0, NUM_FEATURES - 1)
         data[index, feature_index] = random.uniform(2, 3) # Introduce
higher values
    return data
def monitor_network(interval=1):
    """Simulates continuous network monitoring."""
    global network_data
    while True:
        new_data = generate_network_data()
        network_data.extend(new_data)
```

```
            # Keep data within a rolling time window
            network_data = network_data[-TIME_WINDOW:]
            time.sleep(interval)
    def analyze_network_data():
        """Analyzes network data and detects anomalies using K-Means."""
        global network_data, alert_status
        while True:
            if len(network_data) > 20:
                data = np.array(network_data)
                # Scale the data
                scaler = StandardScaler()
                scaled_data = scaler.fit_transform(data)
    # Apply K-Means Clustering
    kmeans = KMeans(n_clusters=3, random_state=0,n_init = 'auto') #Setting
random_state for reproduceable results and defining n_init
                kmeans.fit(scaled_data)
                labels = kmeans.labels_
     # Identify anomalies as points farthest from centroids
                distances = kmeans.transform(scaled_data).min(axis=1)
                threshold = np.percentile(distances, 95)  # Adjust threshold
as needed
                anomalous_indices = np.where(distances > threshold)[0]
                if len(anomalous_indices) > 0 and not alert_status:
                   print(f"Alert: Anomaly detected at time {time.ctime()}!")
                    alert_status = True  # Prevent repeated alerts
                    trigger_response() # Simulate automated response
                elif len(anomalous_indices) == 0:
                    alert_status = False # Reset alert status
            time.sleep(5) #Analyze every 5 seconds
    def trigger_response():
        """Simulates automated incident response."""
        print("Automated Response: Isolating suspicious systems and blocking
traffic...")
        time.sleep(2)
        print("Automated Response: Action completed.")
    # Start threads
    monitoring_thread = threading.Thread(target=monitor_network)
    analysis_thread = threading.Thread(target=analyze_network_data)
    monitoring_thread.daemon = True
    analysis_thread.daemon = True
    monitoring_thread.start()
    analysis_thread.start()
    # Keep main thread alive
    while True:
        time.sleep(60)
```

Explanation

- **Simulated Network Data:** The `generate_network_data` function simulates network traffic data. It generates random data points and injects a few anomalies by introducing higher values in certain features.
- **K-Means Anomaly Detection:** The `analyze_network_data` function uses K-Means clustering to identify anomalies. It scales the data, fits a K-Means model, calculates the distance of each point from the cluster centroids, and flags points that are far from any centroid as anomalies.
- **Automated Response:** The `trigger_response` function simulates an automated incident response by printing a message indicating that suspicious systems are being isolated and traffic is being blocked.
- **Threading:** The code uses threads to simulate continuous network monitoring and analysis. The `monitor_network` thread generates network data and appends it to a global `network_data` list. The `analyze_network_data` thread analyzes the data and triggers an alert and automated response if anomalies are detected.

Sample Output (May Vary Due to Randomness)

- **Alert:** Anomaly detected at time Sat Mar 15 22:25:06 2025!
- **Automated Response:** Isolating suspicious systems and blocking traffic...
- **Automated Response:** Action completed.

Note: This is a simplified simulation. A real-world autonomous IDS would involve much more complex algorithms, data sources, and response mechanisms.

Video Resources
https://www.youtube.com/watch?v=OS9xRGKfx4E

Use of ICT

The use of Information and Communication Technology (ICT) is critical for enabling autonomous and self-healing Intrusion Detection Systems (IDS). ICT infrastructure facilitates the collection and analysis of vast amounts of network data, including traffic patterns and system logs, which serves as the foundation for machine learning models to detect anomalies and intrusions.

Real-time data processing is enabled through ICT systems, integrating machine learning algorithms into platforms like cloud services or edge devices, which is crucial for applications like fraud detection, cybersecurity, and industrial monitoring. ICT infrastructure, such as GPUs and distributed computing systems, accelerates the training of complex models like neural networks and Isolation Forests.

Additionally, cloud-based ICT platforms allow scalable deployment of anomaly detection models, supporting continuous learning by updating models with new data. ICT tools also provide visualization interfaces that help stakeholders interpret detected anomalies, enabling informed decision-making across various domains including finance, healthcare, cybersecurity, and manufacturing.

5.5 OPEN RESEARCH CHALLENGES IN IDS DEVELOPMENT

5.5.1 Evolving Threats Scenario and Adaptive Learning

A major challenge in Intrusion Detection System (IDS) development is the rapidly evolving threat scenario. Traditional signature-based IDS struggle to keep pace with novel attacks and zero-day exploits. Machine learning (ML) and deep learning (DL) offer promising solutions through adaptive learning, enabling IDS to detect anomalies and previously unseen attack patterns. However, research is needed to improve the robustness and generalization ability of these models, ensuring they can effectively detect threats across diverse network environments and data distributions.

5.5.2 Feature Engineering and Data Representation

Effective feature engineering and data representation are crucial for the performance of ML-based IDS. Raw network traffic data often contains irrelevant or redundant information, which can degrade model accuracy and efficiency. Research is needed to develop automated feature selection techniques that can identify the most informative features for anomaly detection and intrusion classification. Additionally, exploring novel data representation methods, such as graph-based representations or transformer-based embeddings, can capture complex relationships and dependencies in network traffic, leading to improved detection capabilities. The figure 5.4 represents the ML models with Feature Engineering.

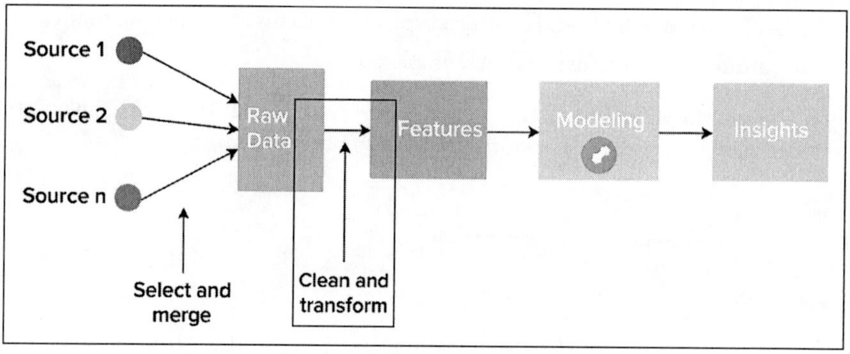

Figure 5.4: *ML Models with Feature Engineering*

5.5.3 Interpretability and Explainability

The "black box" nature of DL models poses a significant challenge for IDS deployment. Security analysts need to understand why a particular event is flagged as suspicious to validate the alert and take appropriate action. Research is needed to develop explainable AI (XAI) techniques that can provide insights into the decision-making processes of ML-based IDS. This includes methods for visualizing important features, generating textual explanations, and identifying potential biases in the model.

5.5.4 Scalability and Real-time Processing

Modern networks generate massive amounts of data, requiring IDS to process traffic in real-time while maintaining high accuracy. Research is needed to develop scalable and efficient ML algorithms that can handle large data volumes and high traffic rates. This includes exploring distributed computing architectures, hardware acceleration techniques, and model compression methods to reduce computational overhead. Additionally, research is needed to optimize the deployment of IDS in edge computing environments, enabling real-time threat detection and response closer to the data source.

Video Resources
https://www.youtube.com/watch?v=OS9xRGKfx4E

Use of ICT

Addressing open research challenges in IDS development relies heavily on the strategic use of Information and Communication Technology (ICT) to enable efficient data processing, advanced algorithm implementation, and real-time threat detection. ICT infrastructure facilitates the collection, storage, and analysis of large-scale network traffic data, providing a foundation for machine learning models to identify subtle anomalies and evolving attack patterns. High-performance computing resources and cloud-based platforms accelerate the training and deployment of complex deep learning models, enhancing IDS accuracy and scalability. Additionally, ICT tools provide visualization interfaces that allow security analysts to interpret model outputs, gain insights into potential threats, and implement appropriate response measures in a timely manner, thereby advancing the effectiveness of IDS in dynamic network environments.

5.6 CASE STUDY: FUTURE TRENDS AND RESEARCH CHALLENGES IN IDS – PROTECTING A SMART CITY INFRASTRUCTURE

5.6.1 The Smart City as a Complex Attack Surface

Smart cities, with their interconnected networks of IoT devices, critical infrastructure, and public services, present a vast and complex attack surface for cybercriminals. These urban ecosystems rely heavily on data-driven decision-making, making them particularly vulnerable to disruptions caused by malicious attacks. Traditional security approaches are often inadequate to address the unique challenges posed by smart cities, necessitating the development of advanced Intrusion Detection Systems (IDS) tailored to this dynamic environment. Future trends in IDS for smart cities must focus on enhancing detection accuracy, minimizing false positives, and adapting to the evolving threat landscape.

5.6.2 AI-Driven IDS for Proactive Threat Detection

Artificial Intelligence (AI) and machine learning (ML) are poised to play a central role in future IDS for smart cities. AI-driven IDS can analyze vast amounts of data from diverse sources, identify subtle anomalies, and proactively detect potential security threats before they escalate into full-blown incidents. Deep learning techniques, such as Convolutional Neural Networks (CNNs) and Long Short-Term Memory (LSTM) networks, can be leveraged to automatically learn and extract intricate patterns from network traffic data, improving the detection of sophisticated attacks. However, research is needed to address the challenges of data scarcity, model interpretability, and adversarial attacks in AI enabled IDS.

5.6.3 Focus on Anomaly Detection

Given the dynamic nature of smart city environments and the ever-evolving threat landscape, anomaly detection techniques are essential. Machine learning models like Isolation Forests, Local Outlier Factor (LOF), and autoencoders are effective for identifying deviations from normal network behavior, which can indicate potential intrusions or malicious activities. By leveraging these models, organizations can enhance their ability to respond to potential threats effectively and maintain high-quality data integrity.

5.6.4 Research Challenges in Protecting Smart City Infrastructure

Protecting a smart city infrastructure presents several unique research challenges. One challenge is the heterogeneity of IoT devices and communication protocols, which makes it difficult to develop a unified security solution. Another challenge is the need for real-time threat detection and response, given the critical nature of many smart city services. Additionally, research is needed to address the privacy and security implications of collecting and analyzing large amounts of citizen data.

5.6.5 Future Directions: Collaborative and Distributed IDS

Future research should focus on developing collaborative and distributed IDS architectures for smart cities. Collaborative IDS would enable different components of the smart city infrastructure to share threat intelligence and coordinate security responses. Distributed IDS would involve deploying lightweight IDS agents on individual devices or network segments, enabling localized threat detection and response. By combining these approaches, smart cities can create a more resilient and secure environment for their citizens.

Video Resources
https://www.youtube.com/watch?v=OS9xRGKfx4E

Use of ICT

The application of Information and Communication Technology (ICT) is crucial for addressing future trends and research challenges in Intrusion Detection Systems (IDS) aimed at protecting smart city infrastructures. ICT infrastructure enables the seamless collection, processing, and analysis of vast datasets generated by heterogeneous smart city components, facilitating real-time threat detection and response. Cloud computing platforms and high-performance computing resources support the training and deployment of advanced AI and machine learning models, enhancing IDS accuracy and scalability. Moreover, ICT tools offer visualization interfaces that enable security analysts to interpret complex threat patterns, collaborate effectively, and implement proactive security measures, thereby safeguarding the interconnected systems and services that underpin smart city operations.

SUMMARY

- **Emerging Cyber Threats and Expanding Attack Surfaces**: The proliferation of IoT devices, AI-driven attacks, and blurred network boundaries have widened attack surfaces, necessitating adaptive and proactive IDS solutions.
- **Adversarial Machine Learning Attacks on IDS**: Cybercriminals exploit vulnerabilities in machine learning models to bypass IDS, highlighting the need for robust defenses against adversarial techniques.
- **Integrating IDS with SIEM Systems**: Combining IDS with Security Information and Event Management (SIEM) systems enhances comprehensive threat detection, response, and incident correlation across complex infrastructures.
- **Autonomous and Self-Healing IDS**: These systems leverage AI to autonomously detect, respond to, and recover from attacks, ensuring resilience in dynamic environments.

- **Open Research Challenges in IDS Development**: Key challenges include improving scalability, reducing false positives, and securing smart city infrastructures against advanced threats, as demonstrated in the case study on protecting smart cities.

EXERCISES

A. Subjective Questions

Category-I *(Revised Bloom's Levels-1, 2 & 3)*

1. Define an attack surface and explain its significance in the context of emerging cyber threats.
2. What are adversarial machine learning attacks, and how do they affect IDS performance?
3. Describe the role of SIEM in enhancing IDS functionality.
4. Explain the concept of autonomous and self-healing IDS with an example.
5. Summarize the key challenges in IDS development discussed in the case study on protecting smart city infrastructure.

Category-II *(Revised Bloom's Levels-4, 5 & 6)*

1. Analyze the impact of expanding attack surfaces due to IoT proliferation on IDS design and implementation.
2. Propose strategies to counter adversarial machine learning attacks on IDS in critical infrastructures.
3. Evaluate the integration of IDS with SIEM systems for real-time threat detection and response in enterprise networks.
4. Design a framework for implementing autonomous and self-healing IDS in a smart city infrastructure.
5. Critically assess open research challenges in IDS development and suggest innovative solutions to address them.

B. Objective Questions

Category-I *(Revised Bloom's Levels-1, 2 & 3)*

1. What is an attack surface?
   (a) A physical location vulnerable to cyberattacks
   (b) The total points where an attacker can attempt unauthorized access
   (c) A tool used for monitoring network traffic
   (d) A type of malware targeting IoT devices
2. Which of the following is a characteristic of adversarial machine learning attacks?
   (a) Exploiting vulnerabilities in training data to mislead models
   (b) Encrypting data to prevent detection by IDS
   (c) Using brute force methods to overload systems
   (d) Targeting physical security measures

3. What is the primary purpose of integrating IDS with SIEM systems?
   (a) To automate network configuration changes
   (b) To correlate alerts and enhance threat detection capabilities
   (c) To replace traditional firewalls entirely
   (d) To reduce hardware costs for cybersecurity tools
4. Autonomous and self-healing IDS are designed to:
   (a) Rely on manual intervention for threat mitigation
   (b) Detect, respond to, and recover from attacks automatically
   (c) Focus solely on signature-based detection methods
   (d) Operate only in static network environments
5. Which of the following is an open research challenge in IDS development?
   (a) Reducing scalability for small networks
   (b) Improving resilience against adversarial attacks
   (c) Eliminating false positives entirely without trade-offs
   (d) Restricting IDS use to specific industries

Ans.: 1. (b), 2. (a), 3. (b), 4. (b), 5. (b)

Category-II *(Revised Bloom's Levels-4, 5 & 6)*

1. What is a key advantage of integrating SIEM with IDS?
   (a) It eliminates the need for anomaly detection algorithms
   (b) It enables comprehensive threat correlation across multiple sources
   (c) It reduces the computational cost of running machine learning models
   (d) It replaces endpoint security tools entirely
2. How do adversarial machine learning attacks compromise IDS?
   (a) By encrypting malicious traffic to evade detection
   (b) By manipulating training data or exploiting model weaknesses
   (c) By targeting physical network infrastructure directly
   (d) By overwhelming systems with brute force attacks
3. Which feature is essential for self-healing IDS?
   (a) Manual rule updates by administrators
   (b) AI-driven adaptive response mechanisms
   (c) Centralized monitoring for all network activities
   (d) Predefined static alert thresholds
4. What is one major challenge when designing IDS for smart city infrastructures?
   (a) Lack of available datasets for training models
   (b) High scalability requirements due to interconnected systems
   (c) Limited use cases for real-time analytics tools
   (d) Inability to detect traditional cyberattacks

5. Which strategy is most effective against expanding attack surfaces caused by IoT proliferation?
   (a) Implementing static rule-based detection methods
   (b) Using advanced encryption techniques across all devices
   (c) Employing distributed and adaptive IDS solutions
   (d) Reducing device connectivity within networks

Ans.: 1. (b), 2. (b), 3. (b), 4. (b), 5. (c)

TEACHER'S KNOW MORE

To effectively teach the topics in this chapter, educators should focus on the dynamic nature of cybersecurity and the innovative approaches to tackling emerging challenges. Emphasis should be placed on understanding how evolving attack surfaces, driven by IoT proliferation and AI advancements, create complex vulnerabilities that require adaptive IDS solutions. Educators can explore adversarial machine learning attacks and their impact on IDS performance, highlighting strategies to defend against such threats. The integration of IDS with SIEM systems should be discussed as a key method for achieving comprehensive threat detection and response across interconnected infrastructures. Autonomous and self-healing IDS represent cutting-edge advancements, showcasing how AI-driven systems can proactively adapt and recover from attacks without human intervention. Finally, open research challenges, such as securing smart city infrastructures, provide a practical context for discussing future directions in IDS development, supported by the case study on protecting smart cities from sophisticated cyber threats.

Intentionally Left Blank!